The *Best* IS YET TO COME

ANN PLATZ

Harvest House Publishers
Eugene, Oregon 97402

499

D0251643

Cover design by Kochel Peterson & Associates, Minneapolis, Minnesota

THE BEST IS YET TO COME
Copyright © 2000 by Ann Platz
Published by Harvest House Publishers
Eugene, Oregon 97402

Library of Congress Cataloging-in-Publication Data
    Platz, Ann.
        The best is yet to come / Ann Platz.
            p. cm.
        ISBN 0-7369-0230-9
        1. Christian women—Religious life. 2. Christian women—Conduct of life. ·
    BV4527.P59 2000
    248.8'43—dc21   99-085699

Printed in the United States of America.

    00 01 02 03 04 05 / BP / 10 9 8 7 6 5 4 3 2 1

The Best Is Yet to Come

is dedicated to

my beloved husband, John Platz.

Your love has added

Texture

Color

Music

Fragrance

Laughter

Warmth

And wholeness to my life.
I am blessed and honored to be your wife.
Hold my hand and walk with me because...

The Best Is Yet to Come!

Acknowledgments

Heartfelt thanks to all the staff at Harvest House Publishers for their love and prayerful support during this project.

To Betty Fletcher and Anne Severance, my editors extraordinaire, thank you from the bottom of my heart.

A special thank you to Kay Arthur for introducing me to Harvest House.

To LaRae Weikert, Carolyn McCready, Ruth Samsel, Alice Evans and the many others who worked so hard, thank you, thank you!

Special thanks and appreciation to Dorothy Altman and Fran Beaver.

And to my husband, John, daughters, Courtney and Margo, son-in-law, Michael, and grandchildren, Ivey, Dickson, Morris, Jonathan, Jeremy, and Jon-Michael, many thanks for your love, patience and support while I was writing

The Best Is Yet to Come.

Contents

❧ Awakenings ❧

❧ The Well-Seasoned Woman ❧

Lord of the changing seasons of my life, There is a beauty, a quiet splendor, in the journey of maturity when we travel with You...year by year, season by season, growing closer, becoming more and more Your servant and Your friend.

Help me, Lord, to live so closely to Your truth, so completely in Your will, that wisdom lines my spirit as time lines my face. Keep my heart forever young, my hope in You unfailing. Let me age in autumn colors, dressed in banners of Your love.

—B. J. Hoff,
from *Faces in the Crowd*[1]

Come Celebrate!

For twenty-five years, my world has been immersed in interiors. I love transformation. As an interior designer, I enjoy helping to transform people's houses. I take a room, add layer upon layer, and help facilitate its metamorphosis into a place of beauty and function.

A few years ago I began to write for publication. I have poured myself into this profession just as I have the profession of interior design. It is rewarding to see how quickly words and ideas can tell a story, paint a picture, and encourage readers to be willing to stretch and grow. I am now as eager to wield words in the transformation process as fabrics and furnishings.

I am a wife, mother, daughter, grandmother, sister, aunt, and friend. As a woman past fifty, I am enjoying the happiest years of my life. I fully expect the coming ones to be even more joyous and productive.

Around the age of fifty, many women experience an intense awakening—a profound clarity and newness of vision. A middle-age celebration!

The Best Is Yet to Come is all about awakening to the wonders of the deeper life. Yielding to the Creator, who designed each life, will enlighten our dreams, guide our choices, and determine our future. As we listen to God's heartbeat and submit to His correction, we are refined like gold.

Progressing toward maturity, we become aware that the earthly treasures we once held dear are in transition. We have eyes to see ourselves, our family, our friends, and our relationship with the Lord from His perspective. We are ready to go deeper with Him.

The well-seasoned woman mentors and blesses all who touch her life. Now in full bloom, she is prepared to hand down spiritual heirlooms and to pass the torch to future generations.

Throughout this book you will find *Heirlooms*, rich nuggets of truth and wisdom, inherited from those who have gone before and a part of the legacy we leave behind. These priceless treasures are taken from God's Word and from the shared experience of other great writers, composers, and poets of the world. Enjoy them, learn from them, and pass them on.

Come along with me, for the best is yet to be....

—*Ann Platz*

Awakenings

1

The View from Mid-Life

Heirloom: *"The only way to be obedient to the heavenly vision is to give our utmost for God's highest."*

—Oswald Chambers

Sitting at her dressing table, she studies the reflection looking back at her from the mirror. The features have not changed much. Oh, maybe a fine line here and there—a brushstroke of time.

But there is more than meets the eye. A patina of the years. The mellow glow of a life beautifully lived. Dignity and grace. Godly elegance. A certain finish. Refinement.

I have never been sensitive about my age. Half the time, I don't even remember how old I am. When people ask, I often have to subtract my birth year from the current one and go from there. After the important milestones— sixteen, twenty-one, and thirty—we are all just grown-ups. Age simply doesn't matter. What matters is what we do with our lives, how we handle ourselves, and what we leave behind.

I can guarantee that you will no longer catch me regretting the past or daydreaming about tomorrow. I suppose that is why mid-life slipped up on me. I believe that God has hidden jewels of wisdom for us to discover along the way, and I've been busy looking for these treasures on my daily walk.

Mid-life is the time to regroup, rethink, and restore. It is our time. We must take advantage of it. If there are children, they are grown and on their own. We have reached a settled point in our career. We have established a place in the community and the church. It's time to slow down and smell the roses. This season has the potential to be the best time of our lives.

One of the blessings of middle age is coming to understand the deeper meanings of life. My family has always been the object of my primary love and concern, but as I have matured, I have seen even more clearly the importance of home and those values that are of eternal significance. I can see, too, the thread that runs throughout families—the debt we owe to the ones who preceded us and those who will come after.

A Lasting Legacy

The Scriptures instruct us to pass on our legacy. Future generations must be told that God is God forever and that He will be with us to guide us all the days of our lives (see Psalm 48:14). Older women are to instruct the younger women, encouraging them to love their husbands and children and to prepare and be "keepers" of the home (see Titus 2:4,5).

When I see a beautiful old piece of silver or china, I think of the blessings that accompany this treasure. With the privilege of ownership comes an equally great responsibility. When it is our turn to pass on these heirlooms to the next generation, they need to be in the best condition possible. Heirlooms are gifts of love and legacy that link us to our past.

Throughout my career in interior design, I have been as interested in families and their heritage as I have been in houses. A house tells a lot about the people who live there. Yet when you examine your own family tree, you can learn something about yourself.

My Grandmother Winnie lived in Charleston, South Carolina. A diminutive woman, she was soft and feminine and loved me dearly. During the season her house smelled of gardenias, and to this day, that heavy, sweet scent reminds me of her. She loved arranging her flowers and always had great vases of the waxy blossoms in all the rooms. When I visited her home in Charleston, she would let me cook and paint crafts, and nothing I did or said was unimportant to her. I was eight and a half when she died, but my memories of her are as fresh as yesterday.

My Grandmother Williams, a staunch Southern Baptist of German descent, lived at "Willbrook," the family farm. She was a schoolteacher before she married Grandfather and had taken it upon herself to teach everyone in her bloodline. Though she was a bit stern and brooked no nonsense, there was a lot to admire about her. She knew the Bible like the back of her hand and could read the New Testament in the original Greek. She was a wise woman, fiercely loyal to her family, and one who held you accountable for every thought and action. This grandmother could have groomed presidents!

From both women, I have inherited valuable gifts. I see a little of each of my grandmothers in myself, and occasionally observe similar traits in both my daughters and granddaughter. These giftings are a rich inheritance, flowing down to the fifth generation.

We are not responsible for the composite of traits within us—God Himself placed us in a family—but we are accountable for using them well. And it all begins with a dream....

Reclaiming Your Dream

Heirloom: *"Nothing happens unless first a dream."*
—Inscription on the
Washington Monument

As little girls, each of us dreams of the future and the kind of women we hope to become. We imagine ourselves as mothers, doctors, nurses, teachers, or businesswomen, pretending to be all grown up. The Bible verses we memorize, the stories and movies that become our favorites—all point to the image of those women. The still, small voice often comes to the heart of a child and reveals true purpose.

At women's retreats, I have asked each person present to remember herself as a child of five or six, wearing her favorite outfit, surrounded by the people she loves, doing the things she enjoys most.

"This is who you are," I explain, "the essence of you." Then I ask the women to write down the dreams they were dreaming at that age, stating what they wanted to be when they grew up.

I watch their expressions as they chronicle their childhood thoughts—some, with soft smiles on their faces; some, with frowns of concentration as they struggle to recall; others, with tears in their eyes.

As they continue to journal, I ask them to list the names of those people God has brought into their lives through the years to help fulfill their destiny. The women write for several minutes. The only sound is the scratching of pen against paper and an occasional sigh.

"Now," I speak up, breaking the long silence, "your next assignment is to record what came in to dismantle that vision, to steal your dream."

There are gasps of surprise. Then the atmosphere is hushed—emotionally charged—as many revisit places of pain. Later in the conference we will pray over these lost dreams and stolen goals. A time for God to restore and heal.

He always does. I have heard from many women who have gone back to complete a college degree, to open a business, or to launch a ministry. It is never too late. Never.

But over the years, what I have learned from this exercise is that the vision seldom changes. We are still the same at fifty or sixty that we were at five or six. We are children still, looking to our Father for the ultimate fulfillment of the dream.

A Sure Foundation

Heirloom: *"And no one can ever lay any other real foundation than that one we already have—Jesus Christ."*

—1 Corinthians 3:11

My own walk with the Lord began in that age of innocence. I was all of six and a half on a sultry night in Ridgecrest, North Carolina, where I had been invited to go along with my aunt and my Grandmother Williams to hear Dr. Billy Graham preach.

Back home in Orangeburg, our family occupied the third pew from the back in the First Baptist Church. Twice before, when I had felt God's call stirring in my little-girl heart and longed to step forward to make my way down front to "make my decision public," my path had been blocked by Grandmother's outstretched foot and a stern look of correction in her pale blue eyes. Later, she had told me that I was too young to understand spiritual commitment and that I would have to wait until I was older. While I listened and nodded submissively, I knew that what I was feeling inside was real.

On this particular night, all the way from Orangeburg, I had heard Grandmother raving about the young evangelist we would be hearing. When we arrived, the auditorium was packed. We found seats in the back and took our places, Grandmother sitting in the aisle seat.

My, but it was hot! The hand fans provided did little more than circulate the hot air, but I hardly noticed as I waited with rapt attention for the service to begin. As Dr. Graham preached, my grandmother smiled and nodded affirmatively. "Yes, Lord," she whispered in agreement. I was so pleased that Grandmother was having such a good time.

Then it happened. Dr. Graham gave the altar call, and I knew it was time. My pulse was pounding. This was the night when I would give my little heart to God, once and for all. Still, just in case, I needed a plan to get by Grandmother, who blocked the way.

I waited until the second stanza of "Just As I Am," and while she was concentrating on the words, I bolted past both my relatives and pushed my way down the aisle, already crowded with repentant sinners. Pigtails flying out behind, I raced toward the front and landed almost at Dr. Graham's feet. I never looked back, for fear I would catch Grandmother's unwavering eye, signaling me to return to the pew. But this was a divine appointment and nothing would dissuade me. I repeated the prayer and accepted Jesus as my Lord and Savior right then and there.

Coming to the Lord so young would stand me in good stead later in life, I would learn. In the meantime, I basked in the love of my family, grew up in an atmosphere of acceptance, and enjoyed life at "Willbrook." My foundations were solid and secure.

❧

A master builder will quickly point out the importance of the right foundation for any building project. A poor footing will not support a building. Structural problems will have to be remedied, usually at great expense. In most cases, it is better to tear down such a house and rebuild it.

When my husband John and I were house-hunting once, I took him to see a charming cottage with a guest house that I thought would be perfect for our needs. He checked it out and later told me that he suspected weaknesses in the structure and that whoever bought it would have problems. My husband was so right! A year later, when I drove by the property, I learned that the new owners had torn the house down and were building a new one on the site.

Laying the right spiritual foundation is most critical. Even as a child I was aware of my need for a Savior, and through the years I have learned to rely on His faithfulness.

A woman who builds her life on Jesus Christ knows that He is the chief Cornerstone. To build on anything but the Rock is to build a house of sand. "For when the rains and floods come, and storm winds beat against [her] house, it will fall with a mighty crash" (Matthew 7:27).

The wise woman knows where to build. "Though the rain comes in torrents, and the floods rise and the storm winds beat against [her] house, it won't collapse, for it is built on rock" (verse 25).

Later, the storms of life would swirl around my house. I would know heartbreak and disappointment. I would be tested and tried. But the foundation would hold.

Nothing But the Best

Substandard materials will not stand the test of time. Consider a paint job, for example. If the paint is inferior or watered down and sprayed on, within a year you will need another coat.

In helping Solomon gather the materials to build the Temple of the Lord, David understood that if the structure were to be a glorious and fitting tribute to the King of kings, he must use the best. David collected several billion dollars worth of gold bullion, and many millions of dollars worth of silver, bronze, and iron. He gathered stone and wooden timbers for the walls and hired outstanding artisans to craft each item.

Twenty-four thousand people supervised the work of the Temple. Four thousand musicians praised the Lord as the others labored to complete the building.

Just imagine the grandeur of this House. Its ceiling overlaid with fine gold and studded with precious stones. Golden cherubim peeking from the walls. Embroidered hangings and tapestries of fine linen in lush colors of blue, purple, and crimson. Majestic pillars embellished with intricate designs—pomegranates, flowering almond branches, and palm trees.

The One who would live in this place was meticulous in every detail. Each minute measurement had been spelled out. Each craftsman and artisan handpicked for a special task. All furnishings described, down to the wick-trimmers of purest gold. When everything was completed and moved into its proper place, "the glory of the Lord filled the house" (2 Chronicles 5:14 NKJV).

But just as building the Temple of the Lord was a costly and time-consuming project, so is building the temple of your life. He is waiting for you to lay sure foundations, follow directions, and put your house in order so that He can come and dwell within you. It has taken many years for you to arrive at this stage, and the arrival has not been without its pain and price. The longer it takes to craft something, the more beautiful the item is.

❧

Cost dictates the materials chosen for most jobs. And while it may seem a pity we have to consider that aspect, few people have the option of operating on an unlimited budget. It is always wise to know the cost before making the commitment.

After my yearly eye exam, I decided to go to a designer frame shop to select something different for a change. Looking over the selections, I chose a very chic wireless frame. Written on the side was #285. Thinking this was the price, I placed my order and paid the required deposit.

When I returned to pick up my new glasses, I was shocked to see the credit card statement was much higher than I expected. I had seen the stock number and merely assumed that this was the price. To add insult to injury, I never adjusted to the glasses. Learning not to make assumptions can be a costly lesson.

❧

Every decision carries a price tag. Carefully consider the possible repercussions or consequences of each one. The cost may be greater than you want to pay. It may take years of pain and anguish to unravel a wrong choice because we "reap what we sow."

A friend of mine desperately wanted to get married. Believing the Lord had given His permission, though not necessarily endorsed her choice, she decided to accept the proposal. This marriage proved to be an abusive, disastrous one, her partner an Ishmael, not the child of the promise. The Lord redeemed the situation by taking care of this woman and her four children, but she was single for ten years while learning to wait for God's best.

A Magnificent View

Heirloom: *"This plan of mine is not what you would work out, neither are my thoughts the same as yours! For just as the heavens are higher than the earth, so are my ways higher than yours."*

—Isaiah 55:8,9

An interesting thing happens when I take on a personal project for our home. The outcome always exceeds my expectations. As the team of specialists comes together— architect, builder, designer—and each contributes ideas, the end result is far greater than the original plan.

This principle also operates in the spiritual realm. God always has more for us. He doesn't think like we do, He is not limited by time, and His plans are broader and better than ours.

A few years ago, after surgery, my doctor suggested that I get away from the city more often. John and I began looking for a mountain house in the Highlands, North Carolina area, where I had spent many happy days as a child. I told my husband that I was certain we would "know it when we saw it."

After many appointments with a real estate agent, I became discouraged. So many little houses with huge price tags and not much of a view.

About a year later, we were returning from a house party in Highlands when it suddenly dawned on me that we had been looking for our retreat in the wrong place. When we arrived in the valley, I asked John to stop at the next real estate office. We spoke with the agent on duty there and told him what we wanted—a magnificent view and plenty of privacy. Within a week, he had located our property. You see, God had a whole mountaintop for us—with a breathtaking view of four states!

Through a wall of windows, we looked out on an ocean of misty blues and greens in the National Forest that stretched out before us as far as the eye could see. Light shimmered through the leaves to create a rainbow of spectacular hues, the interplay of color and texture giving us endless visual variety. It was much, much more than we had envisioned.

As we stood on the land we had purchased, surveying all those vast miles of virgin timber, there was only a glimpse of the vision God had planned for this property. I had no way of knowing that within the year our lives would change dramatically and that I would need this place of refuge and retreat for our family.

From the vantage point of mid-life, we have a unique view. We can appreciate the past with its imparted strengths and struggles—both the giftings handed down through our lineage and the mistakes that have taught us well. With these lessons learned, we can look forward to the future with the absolute confidence that the God who has brought us this far won't let us down now. We can't know what lies ahead, but God can, and He holds all our hopes in His hands.

His plan for you is so much more than you have ever dared to dream. Trust Him, wait on Him, and then anticipate His best.

2

The Substance of Things Hoped For

Heirloom: *"Now faith is the substance of things hoped for, the evidence of things not seen."*

—Hebrews 11:1 (NKJV)

In each season of a woman's life, there is something to look forward to—the invisible that is not yet visible. Childhood and adolescence bring dreams, hopes, and the discovery of identity and place in this world. The twenties and thirties are action-packed as we attempt to "have it all." The forties jolt us into introspection, and we are forced to ask, "Where is all this going?" The pace at fifty slows enough for us to pause and evaluate change, while life after sixty gives further time for reflection and is accompanied by wisdom that can only be attained from years of living, study, and contemplation.

The Test of Maturity

The mature woman of faith knows she has not yet arrived, but never lets a day pass without questioning her progress. When you least expect it, the test of maturity may come, and the evidence will reveal how well you are doing. It happened for me on July 29, 1999.

I was sitting at my desk in Piedmont Center, a posh enclave which houses the cream of the business and professional society of the Southeast. Six years earlier we had chosen this location for my design firm because of its protected environment, some distance from the heart of downtown Atlanta.

Outside my glassed-in office suite, I could see a businessman in suit and tie speaking on a cell phone. He then dashed off, apparently quite upset about something. As he passed, his voice carried through the plate glass window.

"Did he say someone had been shot in Building 8?" I asked my assistant. Fran nodded soberly.

But when we glanced toward the entrance of the adjoining building, we could see no sign of disturbance, and we shrugged and resumed our paperwork.

A couple of minutes later, without further warning, the world exploded around me. A half-dozen men dressed in full combat gear and armed with assault rifles, jumped from a five-foot retaining wall and swarmed the corridor. Crouching in place, they then took a step forward and swept their weapons from side to side, alert to the unseen enemy. Across the courtyard, I could see policemen erupting from every corner, storming the beautifully landscaped gardens with their flowing fountains. Overhead a fleet of helicopters hovered, drowning out any attempt at conversation. It appeared that war had broken out, and we were the unwilling spectators—or victims.

I called for my secretary to join us. We made sure the front door was locked, turned off the lights, and tilted the Venetian blinds so as not to call attention to ourselves. Then, assuring both women that whatever was going on out there God would take care of us, I sat down. In that surreal moment, all I could do was pray.

As I sat there viewing the melee outside, I pondered the false security of the past six years. No exclusive address, no lock and key, no well-patrolled streets had prevented this shocking intrusion. Only God could protect us now.

My thoughts were interrupted by a loud knock. "Open up! Security!" came a woman's voice through the thick mahogany door. "We've been told to evacuate the building!"

Having learned from television reports that several people had already been killed at Piedmont Center and the gunman was still at large, I politely declined. "We'll stay here until it's safe," I told the female guard. There was no telling where the murderer was now or when he would strike again. The best thing to do was to stay put, remain calm, and continue to pray. In the meantime, my husband had called. We had him on speakerphone, and he relayed the play-by-play as documented by CNN.

Only much later would it dawn on me that, with streets blocked off and reporters scrambling for the scoop, it was I who had the prime view of the event. Only seventy-five feet away, through double plate glass, I watched as history was being made.

A short time later, the security guard returned with twenty evacuees from the building on the other side of the crime scene. Several of these were young people, barely into their twenties, who were visibly shaken and grateful to find any port in the storm. As they walked through our door, I prayed silently for each person, refusing to allow fear a foothold in our office or our hearts.

The Presence of God was very real that afternoon. As my staff and I served soft drinks, we also ministered large doses of love and reassurance. I could feel the Lord's arms around us, and it showed. The serenity was contagious, and one by one, our guests settled in to wait out our three and a half-hour confinement.

From time to time, God allows us to see ourselves as the women we are becoming. The unfolding drama that day, blanketed by supernatural peace, proved His faithfulness. It also told me that I was stronger in Him than I had suspected and thus able to comfort those who were not.

When we encourage others, we impart hope to them. Without hope, we experience only fear. We never know when God will use our lives or actions as a role model to the people around us. At a younger age, I would have felt as helpless as the people we received into our offices that day. But I had grown and matured in my walk with the Lord to a new level of security. I was no longer dependent on man's intervention—the police, the SWAT team, not even the private security agency located in the suite of offices beneath mine at Piedmont Center. I knew in Whom to place my trust, and my Lord didn't fail me. The foundation held, and I could sing through the storm. But that has not always been the case....

The Pain of Progress

Heirloom: *"If there is no struggle, there is no progress. [There are] those who…want crops without plowing up the ground, they want rain without thunder and lightning. They want the ocean without the awful roar of its many waters."*

—Frederick Douglass

As I have grown older, I have let go of the burning need to know all the answers. Some things just happen. They're not fair and they're not good, but there is always something of value to be taken from every experience. If we live by faith, we will be freed from the compulsion to figure everything out.

I recall precisely the day I took my first step toward maturity. It was on a Saturday, in Columbia, South Carolina, where I lived with my first husband and two small daughters. A college romance had blossomed into love and marriage, and our growing family was well ensconced in suburban life, when abruptly, my safe little world was shattered. My husband announced that he was leaving.

Unthinkable! There had never been a divorce in the long and illustrious history of our family, and I could barely tolerate the idea of being the first.

Numb with disbelief, I called my parents at "Willbrook," forty-eight miles away, failing to remember that my mother was away on a three-week European trip with my younger sister, Mary Ashley, who would be married in another month.

Daddy answered the phone, and I gasped out the whole sordid story. He responded with fatherly concern, "Sugar, you just pack up the girls and come on home. Your mother and sister are due back today and should be here by the time you arrive."

Somewhat comforted, I managed to throw a few changes of clothing into our suitcases, gather some of our belongings, including strollers and playpens, and corral my active daughters. With my nerves frayed to the breaking point, I begged them to play "the quiet game" on the trip. They cooperated like little angels.

My mother greeted us in the driveway, looking pale and concerned. The overseas flight had been long and tiring, and she had returned to discover that some of the wedding details had slipped through the cracks during her absence.

"Darling, your father has just told me what happened and I'm so sorry. But I just don't think this is a good time for a visit," she began a little hesitantly. "The house is filled with presents, the wedding invitations have been lost, and everything is in confusion. Let's talk to Daddy and see if he will rent you a beach house, and I'll send someone to help you with the children until you can pull yourself together."

Not a good time...Those were the words that registered, nothing more. Without waiting for further explanation, I got back in the car, turned around, and headed to Columbia, tears rolling down my cheeks. Five-year-old Courtney kept patting my hand. "Don't cry, Mommy," she said. "Everything will be all right." Out of the mouths of babes....

As I turned in to my long drive, I released my grip on the steering wheel and slumped over, completely exhausted. What was I going to do? How was I going to take care of the children when I couldn't even take care of myself? Apparently there was no place for us at "Willbrook." *This is not a good time for a visit....*

The pity party lasted only a short time. I squared my shoulders and lifted my chin. *So, Ann, it's time to grow up. You don't like what happened, but so what? You're not the first*

woman whose husband ever walked out on her! Take responsi-
bility for your own life and stop leaning on others. Ignoring
the luggage still in the trunk of the car, I took the children
inside. The telephone was ringing when we walked through
the door. It was Daddy.

He tried to explain that Mother was overwrought and
hadn't meant to sound ungracious. "You know she has a lot
on her mind right now, Sugar. But you come on back. We'll
think of something."

By this time I was so emotionally wrung out that I
couldn't have made it to the end of the street. "I'm not
upset with Mother. But I think we'll just stay here."

He seemed to understand perfectly. "Honey, I want you to
know I'm here for you. You and the girls will not go without
whatever you need. Now, call a babysitter and get some rest.
We'll talk on Monday. Everything will be all right."

I took his advice and went to bed.

From that day, I felt my dependence shift from my parents to myself. I have often thought how dramatically my
life would have changed had I remained with my parents
during this trying time. The outcome would have been very
different. Instead, I left my father's house and the home of
my husband and moved to another city to fulfill my destiny.
That path would hold hidden treasures along the way to
womanhood.

Although I wasn't living in all the fullness of my spiritual
inheritance at that time, I was my Father's daughter, and He
was telling me that it was time to become a woman. Daddy
and Courtney were right. Someday everything would be all
right.

🌺

Real maturity requires inner growth, and growth takes place in layers. Allowing ourselves to be stretched and changed is not a one-time happening or something that is bestowed upon us. It is a process. We turn a page with each day, each moment—moving forward, living, loving, sharing, growing, giving, changing.

Change is a constant, irreversible force. We change even while we are sleeping. When we sleep, we dream. When we dream, our subconscious mind is at work. We sort things out. We open doors and close windows. Even as our physical bodies are at rest, our minds are in constant motion.

We have to be willing to be taught, stretched, pushed, pulled, and rearranged. We have to learn to color outside the lines and smile in the face of adversity. Transformation begins when we remove obstacles that prevent us from moving forward.

In the beginning I braved my new existence with more fear than faith. It would take many years to recover from my loss. But from that point on, I was never the same. The lesson I learned was life-changing: God makes us strongest at our weakest point.

Becoming Aware

At various levels of maturity, there is an intense awakening. We experience profound clarity and newness of vision. We begin to see ourselves as we are meant to be at this time in our lives—secure in who we are in Jesus, and giving to others freely and lovingly. The recent incident at Piedmont Center proved to me that I had come a long way from that young, inexperienced woman whose house came crashing down in one of life's storms because it was not built on the Rock.

The word *awaken* means "to become aware," "to come out of a sleep-like state." My early traumatic marriage was an early wakeup call. While I would need more than one such call before taking the leap of faith into the fullness of womanhood, this episode shone a spotlight on my soul to expose my immaturity. To redeem myself, I threw my energies into the care of my children and pursuing my education.

After moving to Atlanta, I enrolled in the Art Institute and graduated with a degree in interior design, an area that came naturally for me. Having been surrounded by lovely things all my life and having inherited the knack for putting things together with a flair from my mother and grandmothers, I was in my element. With two young children to care for, I was also fortunate to be able to operate my newly formed design firm out of my home.

New Beginnings

Heirloom: *"An empty room is the opportunity for a new beginning."*
—Ann Platz

As I began to help my clients with their decorating needs, I often found myself standing in empty rooms. A room without furnishings lacks the contents to be complete. It is unfilled, unfurnished, incomplete, uninhabited. We all have empty spaces in our lives that need to be supplied with the right contents. To be filled correctly may require that we empty ourselves of the past and allow the Holy Spirit to replace our trash with His treasure.

I am reminded of the couple whose house burned, consuming all of their most cherished possessions, including irreplaceable family photographs. When the husband was asked what he was feeling while watching everything go up in flames, he responded, "That fire destroyed all of the mistakes I've made. When I rebuild, I'll have another chance!"

How many times in life does one have the opportunity of seeing all his or her mistakes go up in smoke? When we take our sins and shortcomings to the Lord, He erases them and gives us an empty canvas on which to create a new beginning.

Maybe He is removing some situations or some people from your life now that need to go. Some rooms are being emptied to make way for the new. My prayer for you is that you will be filled with the blessings and treasures God has prepared for you. He is truly the Lord of second chances. It's never too late to become all He designed you to be.

3

Making Choices

Heirloom: *"You didn't choose me! I chose
you! I appointed you to go and produce
lovely fruit always, so that no matter what
you ask for from the Father, using my
name, he will give it to you."*

—John 15:16

Life is all about making choices—for better or for worse.
Whatever your personal history, all that has gone before has
produced this wonderful now. If now doesn't seem so wonderful, don't give up. The best is yet to come.

There is only one you. You are a Designer original—
unique and precious, called and chosen. In making choices,
you are developing your personal preferences. This process
continues throughout our life. Your home and life should
have your persona stamped all over it—not your mother's or
your best friend's. As you have matured, you have come into
a fuller understanding of all you were created to be.

You are redefining who you are and who you are becoming. Along with this process comes an understanding of

others. Most of the major conflicts in our lives have hopefully been resolved or no longer matter. To fully accept yourself allows you to accept the way other people operate. You can embrace the similarities and celebrate the differences in full recognition of the beautiful balance God planned.

Some of my clients seem to have an innate confidence and know exactly what they want early in life, while others are paralyzed when making decisions. A majority of us take at least until mid-life to trust our ability to choose—whether it be a life partner, a career, or a new color for the living room walls. Alexandra Stoddard, author of the wonderful design book, *Creating a Beautiful Home,* passes on an encouraging word when she advises, "Whoever you are, do not deny it. Celebrate it…Style emerges when you accept yourself."

Personal Style

My younger sister, Mary Ashley, never hesitated to celebrate her signature style. Once, when we were teenagers and experimenting with hair color, we decided to dye our hair blond. A few hours later, we went swimming. Mary Ashley dove into the pool and emerged, a la Esther Williams, her hair a shocking shade of chartreuse!

That night at dinner, Daddy cocked his head and squinted his eyes. "Honey," he addressed my sister, "is there something a little different about your hair?" The laughter that erupted around the table broke any tension we might have felt about our parents' reaction.

Because our parents affirmed us in so many ways, we were able to experience our own personal style without fear of rejection. It wasn't long before Mary Ashley's hair was pink!

Our style as mature women of faith rests in acceptance—self-acceptance and the knowledge of our heavenly Father's acceptance. How marvelous to ponder that He knew us before we were formed in our mothers' wombs, that He sovereignly ordained every day of our lives before each one of them came to be, and that He has engraved our names in the palms of His hands. He knows your name, dear friend! Don't ever doubt that He can order your days and guide your decisions as well. The trick is in letting go and letting God.

Letting Go

One of the signs of maturity is becoming aware that something has to go. It's like cleaning out a closet. With each piece of clothing you pull off the hanger, there are decisions to be made. "Will I wear this again? Will I need it? Have I ever needed it at all?"

By now, we pretty much know what works and what doesn't. We get rid of what has stopped being effective or what has never worked in order to free up space for the future. Some material things have more meaning; others, less. We are reducing the clutter in our lives. We clear out the old in preparation for the new.

During recovery from my divorce, I asked the therapist in a counseling session when I would get over the pain. He smiled and offered a gentle suggestion, "When you get sick and tired of being sick and tired. You need to let go of the past." For some strange reason, these words had a profound effect on me. That was over 26 years ago, and I now see that releasing unfulfilled dreams freed me to move forward.

Transformation begins when we allow the obstacles that have prevented our progress to become stepping stones to the future. It was because I needed to provide for my little family that I made the decision to complete my education at the Art Institute in Atlanta and prepare for a career that has since been one of the most rewarding phases of my life.

In every life there are some scratches and dents. The past can be disappointing, even debilitating. You may have come to the point where you feel you can go no further. Painful memories may be blocking personal and spiritual growth. But renovation is possible. In the Master's hands, you can be healed, renewed, and restored. The healing process begins the minute you let go and allow God to touch these wounded places with His love and grace.

A psychologist friend once shared with me that in observing her patients, it had become obvious that the more emotional healing took place, the more color they would allow in their lives, both in their clothing and in their homes. Interesting.

God could have created the world in black and white. Instead, He used a palette with a kaleidoscope of color. Throw out the drab and the monotone. Add splashes of color in all the rooms of your heart. It's time for a change!

Simplifying

Heirloom: *"There is no greatness
where there is not simplicity."*

—Leo Tolstoy

Picture this scenario. You are invited to take a fabulous vacation with friends. The plans include a stay at a mountain lodge, where there will be many outdoor activities, including swimming and a moonlight trail ride on horseback. The grand finish at week's end will be an elaborate formal dinner.

You would need a huge wardrobe with all the proper accessories, right?

Then you learn, to your dismay, that the host has requested that you limit your luggage to one and only one suitcase and a small overnight bag. What's a girl to do? You can't take everything with you. You have to make choices, good choices to carry you through the trip. Each decision carries a lot of weight; you may have to do a lot of mixing and matching. But the journey is worth the trouble.

So it is with all of life. If you want to be able to go where God wants to take you, it may require traveling light and being ready to move at a moment's notice. Toss away anything that doesn't contribute something significant to your life and the lives of those around you. Think of ways to bring peace and rest into your busy schedule. Look for opportunities in your home or workplace to increase comfort and reduce stress, not the other way around.

A woman I know once attended a one-day conference billed "The Superwoman's Seminar." The very first sentence out of the keynote speaker's mouth told it all: "May I say up front that none of you are superwomen, as there is no such thing."

The conferees spent the day discussing their limitations, learning ways to determine what expectations were reasonable, practicing the art of setting priorities, and gaining the courage to say no. One exercise listed all the jobs a woman performs in her life that, for some, are paid professions. It soon became clear that an ordinary wife and mother wears about fifty hats—excluding an outside job. Nurse, laundress, chauffeur, physical therapist, tax specialist, building contractor—the lists were so long that it was comical.

My friend went on to say that this was the most educational day she had ever spent, including six years of college! Among the useful lessons learned that day were that it is not a sin to buy cookies from the grocery instead of baking them yourself; that no child has ever died of eating cereal for dinner occasionally; and that one must receive no less than five hugs a day to be emotionally well.

We may no longer wear *fifty* hats, but the lessons from that seminar apply to the mature woman as well. As roles shift and we learn more about setting priorities, we will find the unexpected opportunities God has planned for us. There are treasures to be discovered—new friends, new arenas of ministry, and so much more.

Taking Inventory

I have begun taking a yearly inventory of all the appointments and people who required my time and thought each day. Occasionally, I reevaluate. Could I be making better use of the hours and relationships God has given me? Do I need to make more time for Him? More time for my husband? Less for my work? Place more emphasis on the needs of others? Less on my own?

What about habits and routine? Am I willing to change my schedule to make way for God's divine appointments? Remember, some of our greatest opportunities come when we least expect them.

Through my years as a professional designer, I have learned that quality in the home requires choosing well-made items of lasting value and discarding the less substantial. Selecting those things that are maintenance-free or simpler to use frees us for worthy endeavors, wholesome relationships, and more time for personal reflection. Taking inventory of your inner life will reveal who or what is controlling you. As we are able to understand this principle with all of its implications, we may find that there will be times when we have to relinquish unnecessary activities or even undesirable friends and associates, freeing us to grow to the next level in the Lord.

Choosing Life

Heirloom: *"I have set before you life or death, blessing or curse....choose life!...Cling to [the Lord your God], for he is your life and the length of your days."*
—Deuteronomy 30:19,20

With the clock ticking and the world turning ever faster, it seems there is no time—or reason—to bemoan the fact that we are growing older. Statistics show that today we have a larger senior population than ever before. This is the age of longevity. Adults are living longer, taking better care of themselves, and staying active for many more meaningful years. In fact, people age 85 and older are the fastest growing segment of society in the United States.

My eighty-six-year-old Aunt Mae Williams, widowed over thirty years ago, is a woman whose passion for life has kept her young. As an artist, she adored her sculpting classes and continued taking them until very recently, when failing eyesight brought that season to an end.

Yet even her limited vision has not dimmed her optimistic outlook. It is her passion for people that has kept her charged with creative energy. This energy, this overflow of her nature, has been essential to her existence. She loves to be around the younger generation, which inspires her to learn and grow, even in the late autumn of her life. Such women are ageless.

Corrie ten Boom, a Dutch Christian, was a survivor of Hitler's death camps. She saw her entire family destroyed, including her beloved sister Betsie, and lived to tell the world that the best is yet to come. How could she have endured such trauma? How could she have traveled the continents as a much older woman, testifying that there is no pit too deep for God to reach, no wound He cannot heal?

As a child, Corrie's father often tucked her into bed and held his hand against her cheek, murmuring words of love. Remembering the security of her earthly father's love gave her the courage to offer hope to her fellow prisoners in the Nazi concentration camps. She kept her eyes fastened on the future—not just hope of liberation from the camp, but that eternal hope we have in Christ. She knew that one day all locks will fall away, and we will step into eternity with Him, where there is no more weeping, only joy and celebration forevermore.

That same security is available to all of God's children. We can march into mid-life and beyond with hope and anticipation. We may not all be a Corrie ten Boom, or a Grandma Moses who first picked up an artist's brush at age sixty, or even an Aunt Mae, but we can face our own future with serenity, look for the possibilities, and listen for the Spirit's leading as we move to the next plateau.

As we leave one familiar season to enter another, God's creativity and bounty are astounding. Our minds and hearts are stretched. Our tents are enlarged, and we are able to have more of Him as we surrender everything we own and everything we are.

The picture of a trapeze artist leaping from one swing to grab another in mid-air is an image of the faith walk with God. That split second of releasing the familiar to embrace the new is both exciting and terrifying. What if she should miss the connection? What if she fell? The Lord designs this move to enhance the believer's intimacy with Him.

The fear of losing present securities is real. To remain locked into old patterns, however, can create legalism and hardened traditionalism. If the Lord is to remodel a home and a heart, a woman must choose to open the door and allow the refreshing Spirit to sweep through.

Moving On

Heirloom: *"To leave is to die a little; to die to what we love. We leave behind a bit of ourselves wherever we have been."*

—Edmond Haraucourt

I well remember when my dear friend, Ann Lee, died of cancer. We were only freshmen in college at the time. It didn't seem fair. She was so beautiful and intelligent, with all of life ahead of her. Then before I knew it, she was gone. Not long ago I found an old letter, one she had written to me when she knew she was dying.

I put the letter down, stunned by the depth of her faith at such an early age. She wanted her friends to know she did not feel cheated that her life was being cut short, that it had been full and rich and she was content to leave this world. What a legacy she left behind. It has taken me over fifty years to understand what she knew at nineteen—that real life only begins when we are willing to let it go.

🌿

The paring down in all aspects of life will make a difference in the decisions we make. I ran into another Anne recently and was surprised to learn that she and her husband had placed their home for sale. They had dedicated so much time and energy designing this magnificent place, it seemed a shame to part with it.

When I asked her about it, my friend sweetly smiled and said, "There is more to life than a pretty house filled with pretty things. We are moving on."

What she said made perfect sense. By "moving on," she and her husband are making room for the new things God has in store for them. I can't wait to learn just what that will be.

Stepping Out in Faith

Virginia and Bruno are another couple who have discovered God's best. She is tall and svelte and silver-blonde, a former Memphis model who models mature Christian living with flair and grace; he, a former business executive, who speaks with a Swiss accent and gives wonderful, warm bearhugs. Together, they have embarked upon one of the most exciting adventures of their entire lives. And it all began on the eve of retirement.

While Bruno was on assignment in Moscow, he and Virginia received God's call to begin Executive Ministries. They literally dropped everything they were engaged in professionally, and left their comfort zone to step out in faith. Now as missionaries to Moscow—to diplomats, political officials, and other business executives—in an apartment near Red Square, they serve up Russian tea along with liberal helpings of love and fellowship in the true spirit of Southern hospitality.

With the relative freedom of *glasnost*, the Iron Curtain has fallen, if only temporarily, and the message of salvation is received by hungry hearts. God is love in any language, and Virginia and Bruno have seized the moment to share the riches of glory with new friends halfway across the world. Today they live with hearts tuned to heaven, waiting for their next assignment.

There is more to life than amassing as many possessions as possible, or spinning your wheels in a dead-end job, or even doing "busy work" at church. Part of the real awakening that occurs with maturity is that once we have discovered the "more" God has for us, we choose to be busy about the things that are dear to *His* heart and begin to store up treasures in heaven.

4

Listening for God's Voice

Heirloom: *"Songbirds are taught
to sing in the dark, and we are put
into the shadow of God's hand
until we hear Him."*

—Oswald Chambers

My very wise father once observed, "Smart, successful people listen. All the others talk, talk, talk."

Learning to listen is essential to growth—at any age. We need the quiet moments in our life. It is amazing what we could hear if we'd stop talking. We would learn how to manage our homes, where to find the items we need—from crystal doorknobs to what to serve for dinner—and which fabric should be used to upholster the den sofa. But above all, we would hear God's still, small voice. He doesn't shout. He doesn't come in with a brass band. He whispers. He is waiting to speak to the listening heart.

He knows what will delight the giver as well as the receiver; the one who is preparing a meal and the one who is feasting on it; the one building the house and the one living in it. The Lord desires that you believe in Him, abide in Him, rest in Him, and obey Him. To practice his Presence means listening to His Spirit constantly. As you wait before Him, self-centeredness with its noisy arrogance is replaced with quiet submission, and you will hear what He wants you to know.

After a woman hears His voice, difficult life battles become bearable. The sweetness of Christ's fellowship satisfies her longings and provides her with strength to serve her family and the world. There is room and there is time for all the things He has planned.

A woman's heart is God's dwelling place and becomes a tabernacle of worship as she listens to His heartbeat. Then and only then will quietness and confidence be her peace.

Pockets of Peace

Heirloom: *"This is my ledge of quiet, my shelf of peace...my plot of sky."*

—Ruth Bell Graham

Listening involves finding quiet times and places to hear God's voice; to receive advice, information, and wisdom; and to release joy and freedom. The Good Shepherd promises that His sheep will know His voice and that He will lead them to green pastures. The decision for the believer is whether she will allow the voice of the Shepherd to be heard over the babble of her world.

Younger people don't understand the need for quiet moments in a noisy world. While they search for excitement, older people crave stillness. It is all about taking a break, of relaxing and breathing deeply, of savoring the stuff of life.

You don't have to build a cabin in the mountains to find peace and quiet. Anyone can locate a space—large or small, elaborate or simple—to prop her elbows on the windowsill of heaven and gaze into the face of the Father. Whatever the place, it should be yours alone, dedicated to your moments with the Master. It can be a special desk or a cozy window seat, a favorite tree or a bench in the garden. You can find it anywhere and when you do, you'll wonder why it took you so long to get there.

A gracious hostess has the ability to elicit conversation from her guests. She will initiate a topic, then ask others to interact. When you go to God in these moments of reflection, you may bring up the topic, but don't monopolize the conversation. Wait for His response. Bask in His Presence. Enjoy Him.

Listen actively—with the desire to learn and with the intent of sharing.

Becoming a Wise Woman

Some people have so much wisdom that you literally want to sit at their feet and receive. Others have so little that you wish they would ask for advice! I've known both in my time.

Being teachable—having a willing, open heart and mind—leads to maturity. But the process of maturing never really ends. Learning shouldn't stop at any certain stage of life. The most vibrant women I know are still open to receiving new ideas, even into their eighties and nineties. These are wise women.

Wisdom implies both giving and receiving information, knowledge, and understanding. Under the inspiration of the Holy Spirit, Solomon wrote the book of Proverbs, partly to explain the benefits of wisdom. He "wrote them to teach his people how to live—how to act in every circumstance, for he wanted them to be understanding, just and fair in everything they did....'I want those already wise to become the wiser and become leaders by exploring the depths of meaning in these nuggets of truth'" (Proverbs 1:2,3,5,6).

It takes wisdom to offer meaningful advice, and wisdom to receive it. But better be careful. Advice is often perceived as criticism. Advice and criticism are quite different. While advice is the art of suggesting ways to operate in life, criticism can be either negative or positive. Constructive criticism exhorts a person to improve certain aspects of life that will bring success. Destructive criticism insults, offends, and threatens a person's self-esteem.

A wise person will receive advice with a discerning heart. The advice offered may apply to that person's situation, but it may not. Discernment is the wisdom to know the difference.

A friend, concerned over a problem in a relationship, was wondering where to turn for advice. As it happened, during her workday two women, on two separate occasions, shared stories from their lives that clarified her situation—before she had even mentioned her problem! Having listened with discernment, she realized that the Lord was advising her through these women, and the solution was clear.

Sometimes it is wiser—and much more appreciated— simply to listen. After sharing my heart with someone— whether face to face or through the printed word—I am blessed to learn what that sharing has meant. Shortly after the publication of my last two books, I sent some copies to a friend and received this lovely thank-you:

Dear Friend and Mentor Ann,

> The beautiful books arrived today. It felt as if you had reached out and hugged me! What a gift of yourself you have given—and how special it is to receive. Thank you.
>
> One of the sections in *Social Graces* is headed "To Listen Is Divine." That is exactly how it seems to me and to many other women when you extend to us the quality of your listening—intent, intelligent, focused, and receptive is your gaze and your body language. We know we have not only been heard, but we have been connected with, revitalized, and affirmed.
>
> I shall treasure the books, Ann, so filled are they with wisdom and wit. And even more, I treasure you, my friend.
>
> Warmest appreciation,
> Judith

Hearing from Judith after my gift to her was like a gift in return—a benediction on our friendship. It taught me something more about what happens when we love and listen well.

Asking for What You Need

Heirloom: *"Ask, and you will be given what you ask for...for everyone who asks, receives."*
—Matthew 7:7,8

I had been getting better acquainted with God for several years after my first "awakening," so the idea that communication—including prayer—is a two-way conversation was not completely new to me. The problem is that we so often want to do all the talking. As one television speaker said recently, "How ironic that we appear before Almighty God with our list of grievances, our requests, our recital of all that's going on in our lives when He is the One who created us and knows everything in the first place!"

As a single mother with two children and a growing clientele, I sometimes shot up desperate one-word prayers on the run. I hadn't learned to wait in His Presence for the answers. But then perhaps that was because I hadn't understood how to ask for what I needed.

I will never forget the Sunday my pastor, Dr. Paul Walker, was speaking on the subject of God's love. "God is *for* you," declared Dr. Walker with great emphasis. "He wants to give you the desires of your heart. Just ask!" His words pierced my heart like an arrow, and I felt a wave of joy course through my body. What? What was that he had said? That the Lord wanted to give me the "desires of my heart"?

The idea came as such a giant revelation that I sat there, marveling at its power. Never having been an impulsive person, I decided to take my time. I'd search my heart, reflect on the sermon, and try to decide what I needed God to do for me. I knew only that the "desires of the heart" could be found in the deepest part of my being—at the very core.

When I was alone, I turned the idea over in my mind and then began to chuckle. The desires of my heart? At this point in my life, the answer to that question was easy.

At the time of Dr. Walker's sermon, I had experienced a period of intense emotional healing and knew that God would be faithful to bring to completion what He had begun in me. Knowing that my heavenly Father is capable of all things, I felt compelled to say out loud what I wanted most from Him: a wonderful husband!

During the week, I compiled a list of the traits I most admired in a man. Nowhere on that list did "wealth" or "good looks" appear. Knowing how temporary those qualities are, I had discarded them long ago. Instead, I wanted someone who loved the Lord with all his heart, someone with a deep sense of integrity and honor, a man like my father, who would value wisdom and loyalty. Of course, this man would love my children as if they were his own. His strength would be a covering for us. He would fit into my life like a hand fits into a glove. At the end of the week, I sent my prayer to God.

Fifteen months later, I met John on a trip to the Holy Land. When we were introduced at the beginning of the tour, he was standing with a lovely woman and another gentleman.

Seated across from each other at the airport, his gaze was fixed on me, a soft smile on his lips. I wondered what this handsome man was thinking. When we rose to gather our carry-on bags to board the flight to Israel, Ellen informed me that John was her widowed brother, whose wife had died fifteen months earlier. For the first time in years, my heart began to race and I blushed like a teenager. For some reason I had thought that John and Ellen were husband and wife!

The brochure had entitled this pilgrimage to the Holy Land, "High Adventure." Little did I know when our plane lifted off the tarmac just what an adventure the rest of my life would prove to be.

I had been attracted to John's handsome good looks, personable manner, and courtly charm from the beginning, but when I saw him praying with a man in the Upper Room in Jerusalem, I knew I was falling in love with him. Feelings that had long been repressed slowly awakened. Though I tried to resist the strong romantic emotions that were stirring, John and the Lord prodded me on.

As we fell into conversation each day of the trip, we realized what was happening to us. Just as for most people who are falling in love, we were far more intrigued with each other than with the tourist attractions around us, and time stood still. When the trip ended, it was hard to say goodbye, though nightly telephone calls kept us in close touch.

Over the phone we continued to share our hearts. John told me that he had made a list of qualities that he wanted in a wife, and I told him that I had done the same thing, quite some time earlier. We had both asked God to send us His best, and He had answered. That was over twenty years ago.

John Platz, the finest person I know, is the single greatest blessing in my life. God used John's love to heal my broken heart and to draw me to the Father in a deeper way. He is more than I ever dreamed possible in a life mate— God's very best!

Not many of us know how to ask for what we really want or need. But when we spend time listening, we will hear what our heart is trying to tell us. It's time to open our mouths and say the words. Say them loudly. Say them clearly. Say them now!

Listening Brings Release

I have discovered that true freedom comes when I allow no one to control me or my emotions except God. I took a huge step forward when I decided to look to Him for guidance instead of allowing myself be ruled by fear. Fear can be a powerful trap. It stifles and paralyzes. Fear keeps us from moving forward, from being honest with ourselves and with others, and from reaching our full potential.

The Bible is clear. Three hundred and sixty-five times, we are commanded not to be afraid, to have faith, to believe that all is well. As I heard with my heart, I made a decision to abandon fear. I would no longer allow it to take root in my life. I wanted my thoughts, my hopes, and my dreams to be untouched by fear. I was a person of faith, I reminded myself, and a person of faith cannot be afraid.

In choosing to reject fear and by realizing the limitless choices that lay before me, I was actually simplifying my life. For the first time, I discovered that there existed no situation or problem that God and I could not solve. Finally free of my suffocating fear, I realized I was standing right in the middle of a world of possibilities.

Freedom releases us to use our creativity. Creative people have a different approach to life, and confidence and faith grow through experience.

When Claude Monet began to paint in the impressionistic style, it was a startling departure from the technique of established French artists. Local citizens would come to the gallery where his art was on display, point in derision, and laugh hysterically. Some would actually fall to the floor, holding their sides.

But Monet was not affected by their reaction. A genius, he had the freedom to express his talent without fear of the opinions of others. He listened, not to the jeering crowds, but to the voice of the Creator within.

Hearing with the Heart

There is a difference between listening and hearing. Listening is opening oneself up to receive wisdom, information, and advice. Hearing is actually understanding how this information will impact your decisions. It is a "knowing," revealed by the Holy Spirit. To know God is to abide in His Presence so that we hear His heartbeat and value His values.

David, the psalmist, understood how to hear with his heart....

Right up there with the Christmas story, the Twenty-third Psalm is probably one of the most familiar and beloved passages in the Bible. I clung to it like a lifeline during that long-ago troubled time and many times since.

"The Lord is my shepherd...I shall not want...." These words have always reminded me of Daddy's phone call on that awful day when my first husband had abandoned me and I had felt unwelcome at "Willbrook." *Sugar, I'm always here for you. You'll never have to go without.*

Because I trusted Daddy to follow through on his promises, it has been easier for me to believe that my heavenly Father is even more ready to supply my needs. Though you may not have been as fortunate as I in your earthly family, you and I have the same heavenly Father, and I can assure you that you will never "lack any good thing."

He will lead us into pleasant places where our broken hearts and wounded spirits can be restored. He will point out paths of righteousness where we can walk in perfect safety.

Fear has no place in our lives because He promises to be with us, never to leave or forsake us. He will fight our battles, protecting us with His rod and His staff. Therefore, we can walk through every dark valley, completely unafraid.

Like a genial Host, the Lord prepares a lavish feast for us, welcomes us to His table, and treats us as honored guests. There is so much bounty that our cups of joy spill over.

As parting gifts, He sends "goodness and mercy" to accompany us for the remainder of our days on this earth, then reminds us of that most coveted invitation of all—to live with Him in His house for all eternity.

Listen with your heart. All these blessings are for you, my sister.

A Woman Who Listened

During my career, I have often been invited to speak at design seminars and conferences. In addition I lead a group of Christian women in retreat settings from time to time. All this involves a lot of talking. But I'd rather be remembered as a woman who listens.

Mary, the mother of Jesus, revealed a listening heart when the angel of the Lord appeared to her, bringing a prophecy. When she was told that she would be the mother of the Messiah, she did not resist or offer excuses. Instead she replied, "I am the Lord's servant, and I am willing to do whatever he wants. May everything you said come true" (Luke 1:38). Later, when visiting with her cousin Elizabeth, Mary praised the Lord for showing favor to her.

As in any conversation, both speaker and listener are crucial. Mary's response to the word of the Lord was first obedience, then praise and adoration. She knew that all generations would call her blessed because the Mighty One had done great things in her.

For the remainder of her earthly life, she was quick to hear and obey. At God's prompting, Mary and Joseph moved to Egypt to protect the Gift entrusted to them. Later they were instructed to return to Nazareth to bring up the Child. Here in their care Jesus "increased in wisdom and stature, and in favor with God and men" (Luke 2:52 NKJV).

Perhaps Jesus learned some of His listening skills from His godly mother. He, too, listened for His Father's voice and did what He saw His Father doing (see John 14:10). His life's purpose was to hear and obey instantly.

When Mary stood at the scene of the crucifixion on that dreadful day, she heard her Son, the incarnate God, speak from the cross to her and then to His beloved disciple John, "He is your son...she is your mother" (John 19:26,27). How His loving words must have comforted Mary as He released her into His friend's keeping.

Mary's heart was quiet. Therefore she was able to hear and receive some of the greatest messages ever delivered. Through her all generations of the world have, indeed, been blessed.

I pray that you and I can find the green pastures and still waters of our lives long enough to be still and know God more intimately. Let's agree to listen more and speak less. Let's carve out quiet places in our homes and our hearts for renewal and rest.

Jesus knows your name. Be still and listen. He is calling....

5

Serving Others

Heirloom: *"The more lowly your service to others, the greater you are. To be the greatest, be a servant."*

—Matthew 23:11

Some people consider the abrupt and sometimes radical changes of the middle years as a mid-life crisis. I prefer to think of this season of mid-life as a challenge. I believe a woman becomes more secure and established as she grows older. She ripens like mellow fruit. She becomes seasoned.

Part of the reason for this metamorphosis is the weathering process. Over time, we have weathered losses and wins, defeats and victories, and we are the wiser because of them. Dr. Charles L. Allen, the late great pastor of one of the largest Methodist congregations in the United States, once wrote:

> *I would hate to admit that I had escaped defeat in life. Sure, defeat is not easy to bear, but an athletic team would never be defeated if they never went out on the field*

> *to play the game. Be glad for your defeats.*
> *Quit crying about them. Start shouting*
> *praises for them....I cannot think of any*
> *great person who has not suffered some*
> *defeat. You never discover what you really*
> *can do until you need to do it.*

Loss and defeat usher us into the Presence of the only One who can do anything about our problems. Having weathered a few storms with the wisdom imparted by God, we are ready to offer a helping hand to someone else who may be walking where we have walked.

Ministry

For many years after I married John, we lived in relative bliss, enjoying each other and making memories with our children and grandchildren. My business was thriving and I loved the interaction with my clients as I helped them create havens of refuge and peace for their families. Observations on suffering were relegated to the distant past, except for those times when God used me to minister out of my broken places.

One such opportunity came when a new friend, Charlotte, was moving into her new apartment after a wrenching divorce. It was obvious that this move would be emotionally as well as physically draining for her. In fact, she seemed quite apathetic about the whole thing, immobilized by her pain.

To jump-start the process, I spoke firmly. "Charlotte," I said, "this is a new beginning for you. God wants you to live in beauty and order because He gave you an appreciation for the arts. He wants you to live your new life to the fullest, and I am here to help you get started. Now, where are the rest of your things?" Looking around, I could see none of the accessories—the personal collections and artwork—that make a house a home.

"I don't have any accessories," she said with a sigh.

"Of course you do. They're here somewhere. Now go find them and let me help you place them."

Reluctantly she managed to find a few boxes of stored items, and I got out my little red toolbox and went to work. By the end of the day, with her paintings, the aid of some lovely miniatures she had collected, an exquisite glass prism, and a lovely Boehm angel, the gift of another friend, Charlotte was surrounded by tangible pieces that spoke of nurturing love and happy memories.

In time, when she heals a little more, she will be able to reach out to someone else, I thought. She, too, will have learned the lessons of loss and defeat and will become seasoned by suffering.

The Wounded Healer

Heirloom: *"In our own woundedness, we can become a source of life for others."*

—Henri Nouwen

Henri Nouwen has written of a beautiful passage in the Talmud that speaks of the Messiah "sitting among the poor covered with wounds, waiting for the moment when he will be needed." While those around Him unbind all their wounds at the same time and then bind them up again, the Messiah binds His wounds one at a time. "He is called to be the wounded healer, the one who must look after his own wounds but at the same time be prepared to heal the wounds of others."

I believe it is precisely because of our wounds that we can sympathize with and strengthen those who are wounded. As we minister, we make our own wounds available as a source of healing.

Suffering and Death

A few years ago, an acquaintance of mine called my office. This woman, an evangelist, had been praying for me and delivered a stunning word. "I believe that God is getting ready to move mightily in your family," she began. "Above all, no matter what happens, He does not want you to feel that He has forsaken you or that He has taken His eyes off you. He hears your prayers. Through it all, you must keep your faith strong and resilient. Trust Him with everything."

I replaced the receiver, puzzled as to what these words meant. *No matter what happens....*It must be something huge, something horrible. I dreaded pondering the possibilities. My father was growing older, of course, and had some health problems.

But it was not my father who would be taken from us first. It was my beloved Mary Ashley. My full-of-life and creativity, kind and generous, playful and precious, gracious and intelligent sister. The last person on earth I would have expected to lose prematurely.

Totally unexpectedly, at forty years of age, Mary Ashley discovered a lump in her breast. The mastectomy revealed a tumor that had metastasized to the lymph nodes, and the doctors planned an aggressive treatment of chemotherapy and radiation.

With her husband and baby, little Tyler, who was only eighteen months old at the time, her family and friends rallied around to help as she endured the treatments. *Endured?* She almost seemed to *enjoy* them. At least, she made the very best of the situation. Every treatment was an opportunity to share her sheer joy of living another day with nurses, technicians, and the other patients.

She would arrive at the doctor's office, dressed to the nines in cocktail dress, heels, and all the accessories. Life is a brief flame. It is a perfect blossom that soon fades. Mary Ashley intended to celebrate all the days and hours she had left.

There were "slumber parties" at the hospital—times when her friends, one by one, were invited to spend the night in her suite and share their hearts. When it was my turn to stay with her, we laughed and reminisced until the wee hours of the morning. She told me then that she was not afraid to die and that God had assured her that this was an adventure for only the two of them—a very private party. It was a solemn moment, a sacred moment, and I knew that I had been allowed to step into the innermost sanctuary of her spirit.

When her health declined to painful depths, there was one big bash staged by several of her thirty "best friends" at Edisto Beach, South Carolina, where she had romped in the surf as a child. She pushed herself forward and kissed the sand when she arrived, then frolicked like a teenager once again in the wind and the waves. She floated on a raft in the soft Atlantic, fastened securely in the grip of a friend's hand. But even then, she was slipping away from us. And when each of those beloved friends gathered to tuck her in and kiss her good night, understanding that this was really "good-bye," their hidden tears mingled with the salty mist of the sea.

Mary Ashley died at daybreak a few months later, the morning before my birthday. We had been expecting her death, of course, but nothing in life really prepares you for the actual event. It was an indescribable loss. My only sister was gone. From the day she was born, Mary Ashley's presence had profoundly affected me, but her death changed my life.

She taught me that faith frees us from trying to figure out and control every little detail. She taught me that you have to believe there are reasons, sometimes unknown to us, why things occur when and as they do. And she taught me that you can offer life to others when you yourself are mortally wounded.

Because of that kind of unquenchable spirit, God's true gift, we can continue the party. We can celebrate life, not mourn the dead.

She's Just Asleep

Heirloom: *"Why make this
commotion and weep?
[She] is not dead, but sleeping."*

—Mark 5:39 (NKJV)

After Mary Ashley's death, I knew that my gift to my parents and her husband and son would be to plan her funeral with dignity, grace, and joy—as she had lived her life. The interior designer in me kicked in. I busied myself with calls to the florist, designed the program, and oversaw other details, such as the upholstering of the interior of the casket in a beautiful cutwork lace tablecloth, which my sister-in-law Karen, a federal judge, painstakingly installed. Despite the fact that Karen was a busy federal judge, with giftings in the area of law, love for Mary Ashley preceded all other duties and revealed new dimensions of creativity. My daughters, Courtney, then twenty-four, and Margo, twenty-one, and my niece, Marian, insisted on attending to their adored aunt's makeup, hair, and nails. Nothing would be spared for our beloved Mary Ashley.

The surroundings for the service were exquisite. A seven-foot cross in the choir loft was covered in white lilies. Two pedestals flanking the loft held massive white flower arrangements. But it was the pall that paid highest tribute to my sister, whose floral designs for community events were legendary. The casket was covered in green moss with a single blossom of every white flower specimen we could locate. It said, more eloquently than anything we could utter, "Good night, sweet woman of the flowers."

Driving home from the funeral, I knew that the events of the last few weeks were ushering me toward another milestone in my life. It was an epiphany similar to the one in my drive years before—the day when I had felt rejected by my first husband and my mother on the same day!

Suddenly a piece of the puzzle fell into place. That day when my heart was broken and I was weeping bitterly for my own loss, no one could have known how soon we would lose Mary Ashley. She would be with us only forty-two brief years. It occurred to me that the wedding preparations that had so preoccupied my mother and sister, along with their trip to Europe, had been their special time together, reserved just for the two of them. I began to cry again, this time out of remorse for my selfishness. *Forgive me, Mary Ashley. Forgive me, Mother....*

From this day forward, I would see all things from a new perspective. I would take a long hard look at my own life. God was moving me to a higher level in Him, and the adjustment was painful. But it would be worth it.

With time and maturity, we begin to see things we did not have eyes to see. Mary Ashley is not dead. She is fully alive, at home with the Lord. She is sitting down to the feast prepared for her.

Consider your own suffering. No one else has suffered exactly as you have. What lessons have you learned? Will you allow the scars of your past to become stars? Will you reach for the possibilities instead of the problems? Will you permit the God of all comfort to heal your heart? Don't stop. Don't give up. Keep moving forward. And keep reaching out to bless others through your loss.

Refined Like Gold

I once told my father that I regretted the fact that John and I had not found each other earlier in life and that my children were not his blood kin. We had such a wonderful marriage, so fulfilling in every way, that I wished I had known him always.

Daddy adjusted his glasses on his nose and peered over them to look up at me from his easy chair. "Good heavens, Sugar! You'd better be glad you didn't. It's the trials and struggles you've been through that have made you what you are."

Of course, he was right, as usual. It is only when we have walked through the fire that we emerge as gold, purged and purified. My father's words of wisdom throughout my life are one of the richest legacies he left me. For he did leave— only four years after Mary Ashley.

Daddy's Chair

The night he died, I slipped into the den at "Willbrook" to mull over the events of the past few days and weeks. As far back as I can remember, I knew that the overstuffed, slightly larger-than-life wing chair in that room was "Daddy's chair." When my father was at home, he was usually seated there.

All of the family members considered this a place of honor, love, and respect and wouldn't have thought of trespassing—even when he was out of town. It was an unspoken tradition in our household.

Over the years, I have fond memories of Daddy seated in his beloved chair. From this vantage point, he would inquire about the neighboring farmers' crops, make and receive telephone calls, arbitrate some dispute, settle a crisis, and preside over his family. Our most important discussions were directed from this chair.

He died on December 28, 1995 at the age of eighty-three. That night, as I sat in the shadows, I saw my mother pass by the empty chair, then pause to pay silent tribute. A sudden rush of emotion swelled in me as I watched her clutch her hand to her heart. She turned to look at me and offered a tearful, but comforting smile. No words were necessary.

The greatest pain often takes your breath away, leaving you shattered and speechless. It is in those silent moments that God can break through with healing. No words need pass between you and your Lord. But you will know His touch. It will come through the darkest hours—on angel wings.

🌹

There is an old saying that what people say about you at your funeral is who you really are. In that case, my father was a legend in his own time. Over and over again that day, as people paid their respects, I heard stories of how he had offered legal assistance to someone facing bankruptcy or some other knotty problem, often not allowing the person to pay him. Instead, he suggested they do something for someone else. He mentored so many young men and women in his lifetime—from judges and lawyers to congressmen and senators—some of them among the many thousands who attended his funeral. One U.S. senator was heard to remark, "It is just amazing that in the nearly fifty years Marshall Williams served his state in the legislature, he had no enemies. He was loved by all."

Even as a little girl, I could tell that everyone loved my father. He simply refused to have enemies and quickly disarmed the opposition with his courtly charm and grace, winning them over. He was the embodiment of the "successful man" described by David Brinkley in these words: "He can build a firm foundation with the bricks that others throw at him."

This is a trait that I so admire and desire for my life. I pray continually for compassion and understanding, for the ability to see both sides of a situation, for the grace to turn the other cheek. God can use us in a powerful way when we are loving and fair, slow to judge and quick to forgive.

When my two brothers and Mary Ashley and I were growing up, Daddy taught us to respect authority. He always sided with the person in authority, but he took the time to explain why. He was so patient. So strong, yet gentle. So brilliant, yet simple. So powerful, yet humble. Stubborn, too—a trait I have inherited from him. But our stubbornness allows us to stand when others faint and fall.

He was a remarkable person, my father, a devoted Christian, a true son of the South. He imparted so much to me in his long lifetime. The impact of these lessons at this juncture was timely. I understood. My generation was now stepping "up to the plate." How would my life be remembered? What would be the heavenly value of decorating all those fabulous houses? How could I make my life truly count? It was then that God began a deeper revelation.

Another Awakening

The death of a parent is a significant passage. One is never truly prepared for a father or mother to die, regardless of the age. The passage is marked by great sorrow. Gone is the person you trusted to answer your questions about life, the person with whom you may have discussed your inner-most feelings.

Death has a way of revealing what matters most. It is a spotlight that illuminates the clutter of everyday life. My father's death, more than any other, was another awakening, the beginning of a new understanding of my role at this time and where my destiny would take me. I began to critique my life intensely, take stock of where I was and what I needed to accomplish in the time remaining to me on this earth.

Ever the teacher, Daddy continued to make his voice heard, even after death. Things that seemed essential to me lost their power in the larger context of life. I found that I desperately wanted to simplify.

I went home from the funeral and cleaned out my closets, cut back on design jobs, and determined to spend more time with my husband and family. It was my turn to step forward and seize the moment. I felt the mantle fall.

Treasures in
Transition

6

Appearances

Heirloom: *"This precious treasure—*
this light and power that now shine within
us—is held in a perishable container,
that is, in our weak bodies."

—2 Corinthians 4:7

Whatever there is to be said on behalf of growing older—and there is much more positive than negative to report these days—we'll have to admit that mid-life is also an era of bulges, bifocals, and bunions. And do you recall your shock the day you discovered your first gray hair—or those tiny little lines around your eyes?

For those of us in mid-life and beyond, those "firsts" were many hair color treatments and wrinkle creams ago. If we can't discover a true fountain of youth somewhere, we can at least struggle to maintain by doing *something* to keep up appearances.

Of course some of you, like my mother, have great bone structure and a lovely complexion and never look your age. Some of you take the Bible literally and wear your silver hair as a crown of splendor. But whether dyed or natural, every hair of your head is numbered by the God who created you and loves you intimately.

The Scriptures get right to the point when they remind us that the outside of us, our body, is just a shell—"a perishable container," "an earthen vessel." In other words, this façade we try so desperately to keep up is nothing but a jar of clay!

On the other hand, what's on the inside—"this light and power that now shine within us"—needs a conduit for sharing all that we're becoming in Christ. And while we're warned, sometimes sternly, about spending too much time and energy in preserving the outer beauty that is fast fading, I believe the Lord understands a woman's desire to do the best she can with what she has left. Ruth Bell Graham once observed, when asked about using makeup, that she didn't see anything wrong with it. We can't expect the lost to be attracted to someone who looks like she's one step from the grave.

A little attention to the container may result in someone's acceptance of the contents.

Face-lifts and Spirit-Lifters

Heirloom: *"Humor is a prelude to faith and laughter, the beginning of prayer."*

—Reinhold Niebuhr

I am not a vain woman, but when my daughter Courtney insisted I have cosmetic surgery to lift my eyelids rather than prop them up with my fingers, I was enthusiastic. After all, our culture sends a perverted message about aging. Instead of the beauty of wisdom bestowed upon us by our Creator, all that the world can see is the value of physical beauty and the strength of youth—but I needed an eye-lift to see my reflection in the mirror!

However, as one who is in the business of transformation, I was all for aiding the process. I made an appointment with a plastic surgeon, who was a close family friend, then agreed to an entire face-lift after viewing the results promised by the computerized image he made in his office! I had full confidence that the surgery would go well and that I would heal quickly. Still, when I occasionally faltered in my resolve, I would refer to the computer picture, knowing that soon this image would come into being.

Our walk with God is quite similar. As we mature in the things that really matter—being shaped and chiseled to conform to His image—we are held firm by the vision of who we shall become. "We all, with unveiled face, beholding as in a mirror, the glory of the Lord, are being transformed into the same image from glory to glory, just as by the Spirit of the Lord" (2 Corinthians 3:18 NKJV). When the growing pains are over and the bandages come off, we will behold what God has seen all along—the finished work of the new woman, whole and complete, mature.

What we have to do is to fix that picture in our minds by constantly referring to the description of the mature Christian given in God's Word, waiting in His Presence, and asking the Spirit to lead us into all wisdom. This maturing process takes courage and perseverance, a digging in of the heels when it would be so much easier to throw in the towel.

My surgery was scheduled for the end of January, a month that is typically one of Charleston's coldest. John and I planned to stay in a hotel, the Mills House, after the surgery, where I could recover before traveling back to Atlanta.

There I could simply hibernate, not seeing anyone I knew until my face returned to normal size and color.

On the third day of my recovery, Mother arrived for a visit, looking as regal as a countess. She was swathed in fur over a chocolate brown suit with mink cuffs, and wore a brown cut velvet fringed scarf tossed over her shoulders and caught up with an amethyst brooch. She was just as elegantly accessorized, right down to her brown suede shoes. You get the picture.

I, on the other hand, was still unable to wear a dab of makeup or fix my hair, and my outfit was calculated to hide the damages—black pullover sweater, black pants, a black paisley scarf pulled low over my face, and the largest black sunglasses I could find—Mickey Mouse style! Besides, I could have found nothing better to coordinate with the sickly black and blue bruises left by the surgery.

Having been confined since the surgery, with John attending to my every need and bringing meals to the room, I was looking forward to getting out for a little while.

The Barbados Room of the hotel was crowded that night. After we were seated, Mother remarked on how much she enjoyed dining here and that she had seen celebrities lunching at a nearby table just a few weeks before. She glanced about, her gaze falling on an attractive couple seated by the window. "I wonder where they are from," she said in her soft southern drawl, then turned her full attention on me. "But, darling, you are the most intriguing-looking woman in the room."

I had to laugh. Intriguing? That was probably the most flattering word she could pick to describe me. I looked like an escapee from the witness protection program, or a refugee from some war-torn European country, or possibly even a spy!

In this incredible Christian walk of ours, the Lord brings His humorous moments to lighten the atmosphere, or we couldn't endure the race. Madeleine L'Engle, in her fine treatise on faith and art, *Walking on Water,* writes, "Many of the parables make sense only if we realize that Jesus was telling a funny story to make his point, a funny story that was supposed to be greeted with a laugh, like the story of the judge and the importunate widow. And what about exaggeration for effect? Jesus wasn't afraid of hyperbole. What about the camel going through the eye of the needle? Or the man with the beam in his own eye who doesn't see the mote in his brother's? And people accuse *me* of exaggerating!"

I understand. As a storyteller myself, I know what the Master Storyteller accomplished through the use of parables. I could see—even in my cosmetic surgery—such lessons in inner loveliness. The constructed personality that develops for unmet needs in earlier life is shed as we mature, and the real person emerges—the original design God had in mind. Peeled away is the past. Now there is new life, a fresh confidence to be who we are rather than who we are "expected" to be.

My gaze was fixed on that computer picture—and on the image of the invisible God, my Lord and Savior Jesus Christ, who probably had a twinkle in His eye!

Temple-Keepers

Heirloom: *"Do you not know
that your body is a temple
of the Holy Spirit, who is in you...?
You are not your own....
Therefore honor God with your body."*

—1 Corinthians 6:19,20 (NIV)

If we could perceive our bodies as God does, as the temple of the indwelling Holy Spirit, we would have an entirely different view of things. We would want to do everything in our power to honor this precious Person housed in our crude containers. We would eat a more nutritious diet, exercise more faithfully, and rest from our work more regularly. We would follow the Fifth Commandment to "observe the Sabbath as a holy day....For in six days the Lord made the heaven, earth, and sea, and everything in them, and rested the seventh day; so he blessed the Sabbath day and set it aside for rest" (Exodus 20:8,11).

An exercise routine becomes an excellent time to commune with the Lord. An aerobics work-out with praise music, a walk in the park with a prayer partner, or a jog with a set of headphones tuned to soft music or a teaching tape are all possibilities for fellowship with Him. Observing the beauty of nature inspires the walker or jogger to praise the King of creation. Even the very motion of the chosen exercise is part of the rhythm of the universe. As endorphins are released, so are the cares and stresses of our performance-oriented world.

After an illness, a friend was advised by her doctor to walk for thirty minutes five times a week. She followed his prescription for several years and now wouldn't think of omitting this beneficial ritual from her schedule. It has lengthened her days, given her energy she had never experienced before, and provided a guaranteed stress-reliever.

As with many activities, patterns of living are caught as well as taught. If we model a healthy lifestyle for our children and grandchildren, they will be inspired to follow suit and will reap the rewards. I, for one, was negligent in this area until my doctor faced me squarely and told me, "For an educated person, you have not made wise choices regarding your health. You are totally out of tune with your body. You have waited so long to tend to yourself that your blood level is so dangerously low that I don't know how you are functioning. You're not a twenty-year-old any longer." Stern stuff, but something I needed to hear. Needless to say, I got my act together.

In defense of those women who do follow all the health rules and still do not see any demonstrable weight loss—for those who exercise partly to lose weight—let me add that God uses all body shapes to show love to His people. A hug from a more ample woman may be just the touch some hurting person needs—the loving hug some mother never gave or is no longer here to give. It is the motives of the heart that matter. In His Word, God makes this point very clear. "[Others] judge by outward appearance, but I look at a [woman's] thoughts and intentions" (1 Samuel 16:7). As the maturing woman focuses more and more on the spiritual side of her life, her body will cooperate with the Spirit.

Sometimes the Spirit shines brightest through a damaged body. Joni Eareckson Tada has used her disability, suffered as the result of a teenage diving accident, to bring glory to the Lord. As she surrendered her weakness to Him, He has created a platform for her from which to bless millions. From her wheelchair, she writes, sings, and paints amazing pictures with an artist's brush held between her teeth! She is a truly beautiful woman, from the inside out.

Those who struggle with chronic illness must often depend on a moment-by-moment walk with the Lord. He knows your pain—and cares. Even in the midst of the greatest pain ever inflicted on a human body, crucifixion, Jesus was able to look down from the cross and speak life to the very ones who were taking His. You are not alone in your infirmity. Bathe yourself in God's Word and in His wisdom; it will be "health to your flesh, and strength to your bones" (Proverbs 3:8 NKJV).

I have been blessed with good health most of my life, but my few bouts with illness and recovery from surgeries have taught me not to take anything for granted. To be able to get out of bed in the morning, to move about freely, to have an even emotional and mental outlook are treasures beyond price. If you are one of those fortunate ones, give thanks to the One who made you so "fearfully and wonderfully."

For Such a Time As This

Heirloom: *"Who knows whether you have come to the kingdom for such a time as this?"*

—Esther 4:14 (NKJV)

America is not the only nation in the world that majors on minors as far as physical beauty is concerned. Even the ancients in the Middle Eastern culture highly regarded the appearance of a woman. Kings and monarchs, in particular.

The most famous beauty contest of all time was held in Susa, a fortified palace of the Persian empire, at a time when

God's people, the Israelites, were in exile. King Ahasuerus had just deposed his queen for refusing to appear at a state dinner when he called for her. He was not only embarrassed, but outraged, and his consultants advised him to find another queen. But who would succeed the beautiful Queen Vashti?

It was decided that all the loveliest maidens of the land would be prepared and paraded before the king. He would choose the one who pleased him most. This would have to be an outstanding woman, since he lived according to the custom of the day and enjoyed the favors of many concubines.

Esther, a young Jewess who had been orphaned and raised by her Uncle Mordecai, was among the women assembled and brought to the court for the contest. For the next twelve months, the young women would undergo rigorous beauty preparations—six months of costly oil treatments and six months of perfumes and cosmetics.

Sweet and submissive, Esther had learned well from her uncle. While she followed instructions inside the palace, being careful not to reveal that she was a Jew, Mordecai paced outside the walls, waiting for news of her welfare. When she finally appeared before the king, he was stunned by her beauty and startled by her composure. At first sight, he "loved Esther more than all the other women, and she obtained grace and favor."

Meanwhile, Mordecai was living among his exiled people, faithfully worshipping the one true God. When he would not bow or pay homage to the local authorities, a decree was issued for the slaughter of all the Jews. This was the moment of destiny. Someone would have to intercede with the king, thought Mordecai. Esther! Only she, who had received favor, might be able to avert this mass destruction.

Agreeing to her uncle's plan that she appear before the king and request leniency, Esther prepared to sacrifice herself. Only those who were invited into the king's presence were allowed into the throne room. As he had not called for her in some time, she could not read his heart. Refusal to be granted an audience with the king would surely mean a death sentence for her—particularly when he learned that she herself was a Jew.

But years of spiritual preparation by her uncle—a type of Holy Spirit in her life—made the decision easier. Believing that she had "come to the kingdom for such a time as this," she called for a three-day fast among the Jews while she prayed and prepared herself to declare her ancestry to the king and beg for mercy for her people.

Her heart must have been pounding as she approached the throne, but his extended scepter allowed her to enter his presence, and the rest is history.

As Esther used her beauty to save the Jewish race from extinction, so Christian women today must be prepared to face death so that the life of Christ can penetrate all corners of our culture. The Lord is calling women to rise up and be counted. Who knows but whether we have "come to the kingdom for such a time as this"? Our culture is dying. The world is lost, our nation is faltering, and women are stepping forward to answer God's call. Get ready! We must be prepared—spiritually and physically. We have an audience with the King.

❧

Included in our compensation for growing older is heightened spiritual sensitivity. We have more peace, more time, less stress, less bitterness, more gratitude to God, and more appreciation for our fellowman. This joyful state feeds on itself and produces more. Every day with Jesus is sweeter than the day before.

As we become more aware of our unworthiness, we are also more grateful for His love and forgiveness. We can begin to see that even the painful times have been grace in disguise to teach us more about the Lord and His purpose. As our days increase, so does the measure of our awareness of Him. With age comes the wisdom to live—not for ourselves or even for our families—but to glorify the King of kings.

7

Family

Heirloom: *"God setteth the solitary in families."*

—Psalm 68:6 (KJV)

Barbara Bush, the wife of the former president of the United States, captivated the entire country in her well-publicized address at the Wellesley College commencement when she said: "At the end of your life, you will never regret not having passed one more test, not winning one more verdict, or not closing one more deal. You will regret time not spent with a husband, a friend, a child, or a parent."

The family is God's original institution for communicating His love. The ideal of a loving husband and wife with children, grandchildren, and great-grandchildren is the medium for the message. The message itself is simple: Love God with all of your heart, soul, mind, and strength, and love your neighbor as yourself.

Who is your neighbor? Neighboring starts at home. Generally, the people who share your house—your family—are your original neighbors.

A loving, well-functioning family models God's relationship with His body—the church. Respect for individual members and for authority, forgiveness, patience, encouragement, and praise flow freely in a household consecrated to the Lord.

The order of the family—the husband and father as head— is important. This is God's chain of command, His plan for the protection of the wife and children. Submission is not a matter of yielding one's personal authority as a woman, but accepting God's wise provision for protection.

The greatest challenge for the maturing woman who understands and accepts this concept may lie in loving her family with agape love—that unconditional, no-strings-attached kind of love with which God loves us. As our birth families become spiritual families, the curse will be reversed; the broken-hearted, healed; captives, set free; and garments of praise will replace mantles of mourning.

Growing Pains

But there may be some "growing pains" along the way. During our first Thanksgiving at the mountain house, both of my daughters, secretly and independently, went to my husband, concerned about my well being. "All of a sudden, Mom seems different," they told John. "Maybe she needs her hormones checked."

I had spent a lot of time with my two daughters, trying to impart information and values, and like my mother, I hoped they had listened. They needed to be able to think through situations for themselves as adults. Part of my awakening, or what they termed the "difference" about me was the need to push them out of the nest. It was time for our relationship to redefine itself. All three of us had come of age.

As I moved out of the teaching and parenting role and into the role of a mature woman with two capable adult daughters, I was cutting to the point and giving clear, concise, bottom-line answers to questions. They were not ready for that change in our interaction, but it was a necessary part of our growth.

The Lord places us in particular families for His particular purposes. This is one reason why honoring the authority figures in one's life is so important. "To honor" comes from the same root word as the word honesty. Therefore, honor does not exclude honesty. Telling the truth in love is very much a part of God's plan—and the truth sets us free. My daughters are learning that very valuable lesson.

Spanning the Generation Gap

Heirloom: *"What shall we do for the rising generation?...
Talk with them every time you see them. Pray in earnest for them."*

—John Wesley

A boon when growing old gracefully is the ability to appreciate and accept the differences in the generations. In other words, it helps to be flexible. When teens play loud music and choose to dress in funky styles, we can remember our own youth and congratulate the young people on their ingenuity. We can applaud the wonderful habits they are acquiring and go easy on their flaws. After all, isn't it wonderful that they are not our responsibility?! We make the greatest impact on their lives when we listen more often than we lecture.

My granddaughter Ivey's eighth-grade class was required to write an essay of seventy-five words or less, explaining why a grandmother or grandfather should be named "Grand-parent of the Year." Ivey chose to nominate me. Since she lives only three hours away, I made it a point to be present for Grandparents' Day, when the students would read their essays.

I was sitting on the edge of my chair when Ivey walked to the front of the class and began to read: "My grand-mother is a great listener," she began. "She owns her own business and travels a lot. But no matter where I am or how busy she is, she will always take time off if I need her."

As I heard this precious child's heart, I thanked the Lord for the sensitivity to know when to be available to my grand-daughter as one of her greatest champions. I also thanked Him for those times I had had the good sense to bite my tongue rather than speak my mind! But my chief concern is that when Ivey is a grandmother, she will remember what was most important to her at thirteen, and do likewise.

Availability is a valuable commodity. So many young people are hurt and confused and simply need someone to listen. With discernment and prayer, I make it a point to be willing to drop whatever I'm doing just to be with my chil-dren or grandchildren. Sometimes they need to tough things out on their own. But they thrive on our encouraging words and gestures of support—and simply being there.

A friend reports that on a trip to Europe, her grandchil-dren's favorite memory was feeding the birds in Trafalgar Square, with their grandmother looking on. The presence of an older person lends strength, stability, and a sense of con-tinuity to the young. Never underestimate the importance of being there—and give thanks to the Lord for extending your days.

✌

I have fond memories of growing up at "Willbrook," often sitting out on the porch and hearing my father and grandmother discuss the crops, farming, and the news of the day. When John and I built our mountain house, I made sure we had a porch and plenty of rocking chairs for the generations to enjoy as I had.

This mountain retreat is a home for our hearts and was built primarily as a place for our family to gather, a place where memories can be made. We wanted the grandchildren to love going there and feel that it belonged to them, too. In our will is a stipulation that this house must not be sold so that our descendants can come here to be happy. I want my daughters and their children to continue the legacy that we started here. This is a declaration of intent, a covenant of love with our children's children, and if the Lord tarries, with generations to come.

When I was gathering furnishings for this house, I found an irresistible little painted chair, just right for a child. I knew my three grandchildren would appreciate it. At Thanksgiving, Morris, who was a little over two years old and my youngest grandchild at the time, walked into the room. He spotted the chair and immediately walked over and sat down. I was rewarded with the most adorable smile. Morris immediately knew that the chair was for him and that he belonged here.

When we are in this lovely mountain setting, surrounded by the evidence of God's most amazing handiwork, it is important not only to pass on the joy of living to our children and grandchildren, but to impart truth that will provide a strong foundation for their lives. While we are an artsy clan and enjoy working on creative projects—painting, sketching, taking nature walks, and inventing tales—it is what we are teaching these children as we work and play together that will live on long after we are gone.

On Sunday mornings, when we have our own little worship service in the living room, everyone takes part. The grandchildren read Scripture passages and listen as their parents and grandparents discuss the lesson. But everyone is invited to participate, and even little Morris, who can't read yet, offers lofty thoughts on the topic of the day. It is these memories we hold closest to our hearts.

The intersecting of the generations is divine strategy. The older generation is here primarily to teach the younger generation the things of God. Our life purpose will not be fully accomplished until every member of our families and extended families belong to Him. In the meantime, we can pray for each one—faithfully and fervently.

Mending the Fractured Family

Heirloom: *"Don't forsake me, O God of my salvation! For if my father and mother should abandon me, you would welcome and comfort me."*

—Psalm 27:9,10

It is this very nucleus—the family unit—where Satan attacks most viciously, attempting to pervert God's plan. Even if the physical family is out of sync, however, the Lord promises believers that our spiritual inheritance is intact.

For example, God is calling people back to Him through the pain of divorce, which, unfortunately, is just as prevalent among Christian families as non-Christian families. With this societal blight at an all-time high, single moms need to learn that God is their Husband (see Isaiah 54:5), and the children of divorce can be comforted in the knowledge that, unlike their own fathers or mothers, the Lord "will never leave them nor forsake them."

The Bible teaches that even in the midst of dysfunction, God is at work, bringing the possibility of redemption and restoration. Before the children of Israel were carted off to exile, they had committed serious sin, abandoning the one true God and embracing the pagan religions of the people among whom they lived—the equivalent of spiritual adultery. The books of First and Second Kings tell the sad story leading up to the exile. But in First and Second Chronicles, we find hope. In 2 Chronicles 7:12-22, the Lord confirms His covenant with His adulterous people: "If my people who are called by My name will humble themselves, and pray and seek My face, and turn from their wicked ways, then I will hear from heaven, and will forgive their sin and heal their land" (verse 14 NKJV). His ultimate plan is forgiveness of sin and restored fellowship with Him.

God gave us a clear example of family forgiveness in Joseph, the young Israelite who was sold into slavery by ten jealous brothers with murder in their hearts. Through divine intervention, not because of any generosity on their parts, Joseph escaped death, survived false accusations and years of imprisonment, and rose to power in Egypt, second only to the Pharaoh.

During a time of great famine, the ten brothers made the long journey to Egypt to find food for their family. Here, Joseph had been made governor and had wisely stored grain in anticipation of this crisis. If any man on earth had a reason to harbor bitterness and unforgiveness, it would be Joseph. He could have said, "Listen, fellows, you tried to kill me, then you sold me into slavery. You can just go back to Israel and starve, for all I care!"

Joseph, who was in his more mature years, was moved instead with compassion, and he said, "Don't be afraid of me. Am I God, to judge and punish you? As far as I am concerned, God turned into good what you meant for evil, for he brought me to this high position I have today so that I could save the lives of many people" (Genesis 50:20).

Just as Joseph forgave—and our Father God forgives—so we must forgive those who have hurt or offended us. Forgiveness is not a feeling but a once-and-for-all *decision* to wipe the slate clean. As you release the old debt owed by some friend or family member, you will be released from the pain that person has inflicted. And one thing more—you absolutely cannot advance to the next level the Lord has for you unless and until you forgive. Unforgiveness hinders spiritual growth and prevents the fulfillment of all that God has for you. Forgiveness is not an option.

If there are estranged members of the family, our job is to pray and work toward reconciliation. It was no accident that Joseph was born into a family in which his brothers betrayed him. God had a plan for his life from the beginning, which was to save the lives of his family and an entire race of people. Ask the Lord to reveal His plan for your family; then cooperate with the plan.

No matter who your relatives might be or what they have done to you, it is time to bury the hatchet, not your pain. Repressed pain results in depression and physical illness. Pray for those who have wounded you. Write a letter. Make a phone call. Send an e-mail. Communicate. Decide to forgive and let the feelings follow.

❧

On a recent holiday to a resort in upstate New York, I met a darling young couple who had been married only days. At lunch, they were seated with another couple on the veranda of our hotel. I had just stepped outside to get some fresh air when I realized that the newlyweds were having a spat. The beautiful bride had just fired a volley and was waiting, a frown creasing her lovely brow, for her groom to return a shot.

Oh, dear! I thought. *They're arguing on their honeymoon. What can I say or do to stop this? God, give me wisdom,* I prayed, then trusting Him to answer, I sprang into action.

"Darling," I said to the bride with a smile, "I couldn't help overhearing your conversation. It reminds me of a chair whose screws are being loosened, little by little. One day, when you sit down, the chair will crash to the floor. But you may not be able to tell, from the outside, that the foundation is slowly weakening. Don't let this happen to your wonderful new marriage. Build your house with strength and security instead of 'removing screws.' Whatever he said or did, forgive him—and then kiss and make up."

Subsequent conversations with this precious couple lead me to believe I made some lifelong friends that day. At least, I hope I headed off another divorce statistic!

Single Women and Widows

Divorce is not the only cause of separation from those we have loved. Death—the last enemy—claims many lives each year and leaves many women—and men—living in lonely places. There is "a time to mourn," of course, and we should not cut short the time necessary for grieving loss.

Yet singleness and widowhood can be viewed as blessings from the Lord. After saying good-bye to a mate and allowing herself enough time to work through her pain, the mature woman will come to realize that God has not abandoned her and that she can face the future with confidence and serenity. She will discover new vistas of opportunity for ministry to others, new strength and vigor, greater gratitude for her blessings, and greater faith as she leans on the Lord instead of her earthly husband. She will discover that she is not half of another person, but whole in Jesus Christ.

The authority that comes from the pain of walking solo equips a woman to empower other women. They can see in her a new dimension of peace. The practice of God's Presence enfolds her days with grace and her words with strength and wisdom. God's covenant of joy is secure in her heart. She can sing and rejoice. She can move on with her life, unafraid.

Take comfort in these words of promise from Isaiah 54:

> She who was abandoned has more blessings now than she whose husband stayed! Enlarge your house; build on additions; spread out your home! For you will soon be bursting at the seams!...
>
> With everlasting love I will have pity on you....For the mountains may depart and the hills disappear, but my kindness shall not leave you. My promise of peace for you will never be broken....
>
> I will rebuild you on a foundation of sapphires and make the walls of your houses from precious jewels. I will make your towers of sparkling agate, and your gates and walls of shining gems....Your enemies will stay far away; you will live in peace....This is the heritage of the servants of the Lord. This is the blessing I have given you.
>
> —verses 1-3,8,10-12,14,17

As the elderly widow, Anna, prayed in the temple until she saw the Messiah with her own eyes (see Luke 2:36-38), so single women and widows can serve the Lord mightily. With more freedom to move about in ministry, seasoned by pain and grief, they can be powerful intercessors, ushering in a new kingdom era.

Places of the Heart

One of the first things I consider when working with a new client is the family living spaces; that is, where the family is actually going to live in their house. These spaces of family intimacy are the true heart of the home—where the family gathers in the good times as well as in times of trouble and need. These are sacred places that invite sharing, love, and dreams and where parents teach their children about loving God and each other.

When I was growing up, the gathering place in our home was the table in our kitchen at "Willbrook." It was a large rectangular pine table with long benches on both sides. Each generation has gathered around that table and scrunched together to find their place. We didn't want to miss out on either the good food or the fellowship in this room.

Mealtime is one of the few times that a family can sit down together and talk over the events of the day. Yet this precious time is now in jeopardy as our lives become more cluttered with sports activities, meetings, and other less significant events than being together with the people we love most in the world.

My office manager, Dorothy, came to work one day with a sobering story. "I'm turning over a new leaf," she said. "I'm going to have to start cooking meals at home for my family." She went on to explain that she had gone to the drive-up window at the bank with her two-year-old son. When she rolled down the window to speak to the teller, the toddler shouted, "Large fries, small fries, and a Coke, pwease!"

Dorothy suddenly had a revelation that the poor baby thought all food came in sacks, handed to you through car windows by smiling ladies. I didn't know whether to laugh or to cry. While we chuckled at the childish observation, we were all struck by the sad fact that our society is becoming increasingly less family-oriented.

With the turn of another century, many believe that gracious living will be a thing of the past and that junk foods, drive-through restaurants, and microwave meals may have already replaced the lovely sit-down dinners our mothers and grandmothers prepared and served on starched white linens. That kinder, gentler era is not necessarily over—not if you and I decide to do something about it.

Our role as maturing women is to draw the family closer together for memory-making moments, and to encourage the younger women to make their homes a priority. I have such fond memories of Sunday dinners at "Willbrook" when my Grandfather Shecut was present. These traditions are much more than nostalgic trips down Memory Lane; they are vital to the bonding of a family.

Start your own traditions. Demonstrate to your daughters and granddaughters the value of preserving memories by serving a family dinner on Sunday or some other time when all family members can be present. Consider framing your ancestors' photographs and making lovely groupings for your family to enjoy. Don't put those old pictures away in an album to sit on a shelf and turn yellow with age. Speak of those who have gone before with respect and tell your family saga so that future generations will know and appreciate their heritage.

Family Reunion

Heirloom: *"Just think of...waking up*
in glory and finding it home!"

—Don Wyrtzen

While the mature woman is sandwiched between the generations, often caring for both grandchildren and elderly parents sometime during this phase, she is also the beneficiary of the blessing of being needed. At no time is this more evident than during family reunions, when she may take on multiple roles—mother, daughter, grandmother, sister, aunt, and coordinator—all in one! But what could be more exhilarating than a gathering with so many branches of the family tree coming together in one merry mix of personalities and temperaments, something like an eclectic blend of plaids and paisleys in the family room?

My editor, Anne Severance, tells of a reunion she helped orchestrate several years ago at the farm of her daughter and son-in-law. Relatives converged from all four corners of the earth, it seemed, bringing homemade pies and cakes and other delicious edibles. Since the "Barn" accommodated sixteen or twenty overnight guests and other family members lived in the vicinity, there were welcome "stations" for all.

On a chilly October evening, after a feast spread out on long tables that groaned beneath their bounty, the family gathered in the great room. A fire blazed in the fireplace, sending sparks sputtering onto the stone hearth. Mothers rocked drowsy infants, heavy-eyed with sleep. Aunts and uncles and cousins, brothers and sisters, newly reunited, sat in clusters. They filled all the available spaces—lounge chairs, sofas, and even some antique pews, rescued from an old church building.

The low hum of conversation, punctuated by childish shrieks from the adjoining loft, came to a halt as someone signaled for quiet. The patriarch of the clan stepped forward, his silvery head catching the firelight like a halo. He took his place in a rocking chair, plump with pillows, accepted an afghan to ward off the chill, and opened a big Bible.

Almost as if on cue, most of the children crept nearer and found places on quilts spread on the floor or sat in their parents' laps.

Boompop, his glasses riding on the bridge of his nose, looked out over his youthful "congregation" and began to talk about his boyhood years and how he had asked Jesus to come into his heart when he was "about your age, Jonathan." How he'd never felt lonely or afraid since, not even during World War II. He talked on, holding the attention of everyone in the room.

Then he asked permission to give them a special gift. Eyes wide, the children leaned closer to see what it would be—this far from Christmas.

> The Lord bless you and keep you;
> The Lord make His face shine upon you, and be
> gracious to you;
> The Lord lift up His countenance upon you, and
> give you peace.
>
> Numbers 6:24-26 (NKJV)

You could have heard a pin drop, my editor says. Everyone loved Boompop, and these words, read from the pages of the Bible, were filled with love for all his descendants. And then he prayed—a moving prayer, spoken over the catch in his throat. One and all, large and small, received the blessing that night.

Not many months afterward, Boompop went Home to another Reunion. This is a Reunion to which all those who love the Lord are invited. It will be the beginning of eternity.

8

Friends

Heirloom: *"Many people will walk in and out of your heart, but only true friends will leave footprints on your heart."*

—Anonymous

A woman's heart is designed for intimate companionship—not just with the man she married or with blood relatives, but with the people she meets and matches on many other levels. We call these companions of the heart—*friends*.

Sometimes a family member just can't understand the sudden need of a grown woman to laugh or cry over practically nothing at all. It takes another female—preferably one who shares a common bond in Christ—with whom to make special memories, to learn and to grow. With that kind of friend, we can go from riotous to reverent in a heartbeat.

In their delightful book, *Friends Through Thick and Thin*, Peggy Benson, Sue Buchanan, Gloria Gaither, and Joy MacKenzie write of their lifelong friendship. Peg says of Joy,

This girl (she will always be a girl to me) brightens my life! She sees the world through the eyes of a child, and I hope she never grows up. The simple pleasure of being together is all we need to have a good time. Often we spend our days laughing and being silly; sometimes we cry. The important thing is that there are no instructions, no "ought-tos" or "shouldn'ts." No lessons, no rules. We just are....

We've told each other many secrets, and never once have I been concerned about her keeping my confidence. She is totally trust-worthy—a genuine friend....Through the years, Joy has prayed for me, energized me, believed in me, nudged me. If you want to know the truth, she has shoved me! She saw something in me years ago that I didn't have confidence to see for myself. When I think of her influence in my life, I remember the quote from a little boy who wrote of his teacher, "My teacher thought I was better than I was, and so I was."

It is that kind of friend we have in Jesus. It is that kind of friend I want to be. And hopefully, at least occasionally, I am.

My friend Mary, who was suffering from clinical depression, could barely function before early afternoon. When she received a telephone call from her sister in a distant city informing her that she would be coming for a three-week visit, Mary turned to me. "Help!" was all I heard on the other end of the telephone line.

I tried to calm her. "Don't panic. I'll be there in the morning and we'll cook, and fluff your house."

Little did I know that my friend had become so depressed and dysfunctional that her artwork had been leaning against the wall for over two years. She was so overwhelmed with life that she was immobilized. We had to clean before we could decorate!

Saying a silent prayer, we dived in. I gave Mary the job of washing all her towels and sheets, which were piled in a heap on the laundry room floor. While she was doing the wash, I vacuumed her floors and rearranged her furniture. As I hung her artwork, I prayed for a special measure of creativity.

By late afternoon, her house was becoming a home. We sent Mary's teenaged daughter out to buy light bulbs and dimmers to create an evening ambiance. This is like the loaves and fishes, I thought to myself. Nothing much to work with, yet it keeps on coming. When Mary's sister arrived late the next afternoon, she was lavish in her praise.

My friend had moved into her house, but she had never put down roots and made it a real home. As my sister would say, Mary had let her garden "go to seed." The weeds had choked out almost every flower except that of friendship. My "decorating visit" gave her a jump-start. Now I am praying that she'll see her own potential and bloom where she is planted.

You may know someone like Mary. When you see her withering on the vine, not moving forward in God's purpose for her life, use your talents and creativity to weed her garden. That's what friends are for.

Friends Are for Fun

Peggy Benson isn't the only mature woman who understands fun and friendship. I love adventure! Sometimes we mature women just want to do something for the sheer joy of doing it together.

Take for example my darling friend Susan, with whom I have co-authored five books. Of course, it all started with a project—a decorating project. She and I were furnishing her new apartment in Atlanta when she met her future husband. Upon hearing that he would be returning to see her in two weeks, our decorating schedule took on a frenzied pace. I wanted Susan to be settled in her home so that she could relax and enjoy the visit.

I made emergency calls to my workroom contacts, begging for personal favors and priority status. The painters quickly finished up the rooms, and we found ourselves moving the furniture in almost as they were cleaning the brushes.

When the living room furniture was placed and the artwork installed, we discovered that we still had a huge blank wall behind her piano. What that wall needed was a large, dramatic painting. After assessing the situation, we sprang into action.

With our budget depleted, we decided to paint the piece ourselves. We called the art supply store and ordered a five-foot-square stretched canvas. Then, using acrylic paints instead of oils for fear that oils would not be dry when her beau arrived in three days, we tackled our project. We needed *instant* art!

I had brought along a book with an abstract painting for us to copy, and Susan provided little two-inch rollers to apply the paint. Reminding ourselves to "Think drama!", we proceeded to create our masterpiece. I signed the painting with small red X's and O's (for "love and kisses") instead of our signatures.

I must admit—the end result was fabulous! Another friend of Susan's, who later saw the painting, wanted to buy it. It was definitely *not* for sale. This was a labor of love—all the way around. And we had such fun doing it!

Never be afraid to take a risk or to do something adventurous with a friend. As we plant, depositing love in the life of a friend, so shall we reap.

The Fragrance of Friendship

Heirloom: *"There is a sweet, wholesome fragrance in our lives. It is the fragrance of Christ within us, an aroma to both the saved and the unsaved."*

—2 Corinthians 2:15

Friends are gifts from God who come in and out of our homes and lives with special messages. Pay attention to the people in your life. God is up to something. His ways are higher than ours, and He knows the overall plan. Therefore, observe those He has placed around you. They come in all shapes and sizes and with distinctive flavors and fragrances.

In my home, I have a very large blue and white Oriental decorative bowl where I save the flowers from arrangements that are sent to me from people I love. When the flowers are post-bloom, I snip the blossoms from their stems and place them in a bowl. It has become my personal blend of pot-pourri, created by friendship.

My grandson, Dickson, helped me see the deeper lesson of the friendship bowl when he was just three. I had brought some jonquil bulbs home from a trip to Holland, and they were blooming, bold and brilliant, at my doorstep. When Dickson and his parents arrived for a visit, he spotted the blooms, and before his mother could grab him, he had yanked them from their stems.

When I answered the door, there was Dickson, his enormous brown eyes peeking through platinum blond bangs, and holding out a bouquet of my prized flowers. "These are for you, Grammy," he announced with pleasure and pride.

I took a deep breath, forced a smile, and leaned over to kiss him. "Thank you, darling," I said.

Later, as I was placing the jonquils in the friendship bowl, I realized how touching it was to have Dickson think immediately of me when he saw the beautiful yellow flowers. How much love was contained in the little boy's gift. Instead of providing only a few weeks' enjoyment in the garden, those flowers were preserved by Dickson for my friendship bowl enriching my collection of deeper lessons.

As believers we, too, are the "fragrance of Christ." On the last morning of a recent conference where I was speaking, I was wrapping up a teaching on forgiveness. I explained to the women that they would now be able to return to their homes and churches and impact their world with the fragrance of Christ. I suggested that each woman present silently identify her favorite flower and think about the joy that fragrance gave her.

In closing, I asked the women to form a line and come forward to receive anointing with oil and prayer that the Lord would bring forth the fragrances of their choice. God is so good! He astounded us all with His work that day. As I prayed, the Lord literally released the fragrance of each flower—gardenia, magnolia, rose, lily, lilac, and many others.

By the time about two dozen women had passed through the line, the entire room smelled of the bouquet of their lives—the mingled aromas reminiscent of wedding flowers! How appropriate for His people—the Bride of Christ.

Later, I learned that as each woman traveled home in her car, she retained that fragrance for the entire trip. Those women will never be the same after experiencing that super-natural act of God's love as a benediction on our weekend retreat.

God does give us a fragrance that draws the world to us. Be aware that others are looking on as you live your life before them—and catching a whiff of that heavenly aroma of Christ.

Sandpaper People

God, who is building His tabernacle in our hearts, has a reason for every person He permits to touch our lives. Even the "sandpaper people" are designed for a purpose—to smooth the rough surfaces of our spirits and shape us for something the Lord has for us to do or to be. These people are extremely important; they can teach valuable lessons—if we'll let them. As we ask God to reveal His plan, we come to understand how we are to respond.

In those friendships where pain is involved, allow the Lord to heal and help you work through your differences. Such grief work brings personal satisfaction and the sense of pleasing Him. As the wounds heal, the friendship may grow stronger, or it may lie fallow for a season, then spring up from a cold, hard place to bud all over again.

At other times, it is best to move on to other ground. John, in the fifteenth chapter of his Gospel, describes a gardener who prunes and cuts away growth in order for new growth to appear. The pruning is painful, and friends may be baffled when they are separated. But we can trust that our faithful Father is preparing the soil to produce greater love, joy, and peace.

Often the cutting away is the severing of unproductive or destructive friendships. "Friendship with the world is enmity with God," says James 4:44. The world panders to self-promotion, greed, and selfish desires, while God is after righteousness and truth. Believers must beware of buddying up to the world's system. Glitz and glamor are appealing, but God prefers purity and simplicity.

Still other "sandpaper people" are in our lives to stay—either because we are related to them or because God has placed them there and we're "stuck" with them. They are the "irregular" people, the impossible people. People who always seem to need to have the last word. In these cases it may be helpful to remember that there are no coincidences with God and that no matter what the circumstances, there is always a deeper work going on. When we've said all we can say and done all we know to do, we can pray for wisdom to discern what God may be doing through these difficult people and for grace to extend the same kind of mercy He extends to us. It may be time to step back and allow God to bring someone across their path who can communicate His truths to them. Nothing is impossible with Him, and even sandpaper people themselves can be smoothed and shaped to become all that He has designed them to be. Not only that, but these very people may be the cause of your promotion to the next level God has for you—if you pass the test of kindness and unconditional love.

The world is watching. They will know we are Christians by the love we demonstrate in our daily lives. A friend was attracted to Christianity as a lifestyle when she observed the joy her newly converted sister and her best friend were experiencing. My friend had never witnessed such life and love and wanted it for herself. She was drawn to her sister's new walk because she could see the evidence in that joyful relationship.

But it is even more convicting when hostile relationships are transformed and two people who once couldn't stand the sight of each other now relate in friendship and harmony.

Seasons of the Heart

Friendships may span a lifetime or be designed for a season. You will know when the time together is over or a relationship is shifting.

One friend knew that her time was up with a certain mentor. It grieved her to think that she would not be seeing this dear woman as often as in the past. However, if my friend had refused to let go and move on with the Lord, she would have missed some of His greatest blessings. Now when the two women meet, their sharing is richer and deeper than before.

A picture of the separating of friends is illustrated in the tulip bulb. When the bulb is separated and planted in different soils, more ministries can flourish, more gifts can operate, and more of the Lord can be experienced. This separation may come through a move, through death, or simply because one is now moving in different circles. But separation can be positive.

❧

Some friendships are intended for a single purpose only—but a purpose with such significance that only eternity will reveal the extent. It is these friends who make the most dramatic difference in our lives—or we, in theirs.

While I was busy working at the design center one day, I ran into a woman I had known socially, though not intimately. Janice looked exhausted. She explained that her husband Bob was in a nearby hospital's Intensive Care Unit, in the last stages of cancer. She had stepped out to take a breather and to transact some necessary business.

"You may not believe it now, Ann, but there may come a time when you will want to let your husband go...." Though she did not describe Bob's suffering, I could imagine what agony he must be enduring. It was written in the lines of fatigue on her face.

John and I knew Bob only as a charming, handsome man, now retired, who had formerly served our country as an ace Naval pilot and had been highly decorated for his heroism in the line of duty. The kind of man who appears unapproachable because of his commanding presence. Even though I did not know Janice well, I was impressed to ask if Bob knew the Lord. She replied with a little smile and mentioned the name of the church they attended. I got the idea.

As soon as she left I called my husband, told him the situation, and asked him to make a visit to the hospital. Within the hour John was at the dying man's bedside, praying with him to receive Jesus as his Savior. John later told me that it had been so incredibly easy. There was no resistance when he explained the plan of salvation, and Bob prayed the sinner's prayer and was saved on the spot.

About a month later, Bob went home to be with the Lord. Janice later confided to me that her husband had referred to John as his "best friend," the only man who had come to him in his greatest hour of need with the message of eternity.

Friendships cannot be evaluated in time spent together. That day John and Bob became brothers in Christ in a matter of minutes. Bob left this life to join his new Friend and Savior in heaven, and John, too, was blessed.

You are being molded for eternal purposes. Each friend you meet—however long the season of your friendship—will supply you with some necessary building block in your personality or serve to refine you for even greater work. Be prepared to embrace the changes these friends will generate.

I Have Called You Friends

Heirloom: *"I have called you friends, for all things that I heard from my Father I have made known to you."*

—John 15:15 (NKJV)

Hollowed deep by years of painful life lessons, the heart of a mature woman is a reservoir of love. She can love because she has been loved by her Best Friend—Jesus. Her walk with Him—studying the words He spoke while traveling the dusty roads of Galilee, examining the way He treated others, knowing that He loves her even when she's most unlovable—has taught her what true friendship looks like and feels like. It's a hug when she's hurting, a promise to be there when she's lonely, a light for all the dark corners of her life. As she has received, so she can give.

The example of a godly woman inspires another to go on living after the death of a loved one. To press for all God has created us to be, to share enthusiasm about what He is doing in us and in the world around us, to feed on each other's ideas and ministries produces growth and life. Friends encourage and strengthen one another. Friends love one another. Friends pray for one another. We catch a glimpse of

God with flesh on when others stand in the gap and intercede for us.

It is hoped that the hospitality of a church will show the outside world how truly loving relationships ought to work. Koinonia—the fellowship of believers—implies two people in a boat, bound for a distant shore. To survive a storm, they must cooperate. To explore new waters without going in circles, they must row together. There is no place in that boat for strife and disharmony. Our Master has told us that we are going to the other side. We might as well enjoy the journey.

In New Testament days, the women who were among Jesus' most faithful followers walked closely with Him. They were not cowering in the distance on the day He died, but were in the forefront, grieving at the foot of the cross. They were also first at the tomb on Resurrection morning. It was to Mary Magdalene that Jesus announced His victory over death, just as the other Mary had heard the angelic announcement that her womb was to cradle the King of kings, bringing Him forth into human history.

These are fabulous days in which to be alive! Women in ministry—whether as pastors or retreat leaders or voices of prophecy—are growing in number and spirit. Our Lord has called us His friends. Perhaps we are to be the women—or "womb-men"—who usher in His second coming! There is no time for boredom or bridge, for majoring on minors, for sitting back when we need to be standing up. Let's get busy with kingdom concerns. Let's listen more and pray more and wait more. When we are sure we have heard His voice, then let's be ready to move forward—together—hand in hand and heart-to-heart.

9

Home

Heirloom: *"Mid pleasure and
palaces though we may roam, Be it ever so
humble, there's no place like home."*
—John Howard Payne

A home is much more than four walls and a roof or a
showcase for lovely fabrics and fine furnishings. Home is more
than a hotel for people who pass in the night with barely
enough time to mumble "hello" before dashing off to the
next activity. A true home is a haven for the heart, a hospital
for the hurting, an institution of "higher" learning for the
family who lives there. Home is the cradle of life that begins
on earth and extends into eternity.

The home environment provides a vehicle for God's plan
for people to be hammered out in daily living. He created the
home—first in Eden—where love could abound, forgiveness
could be offered and received, and families could grow together in the Lord. Sadly, the first couple failed miserably,
leaving a legacy of shame and sin to plague the rest of human
history. Happily, that was not the end of the story.

A home base is more crucial than ever to the security of people living in a disjointed and isolated culture. Despite the fact that we live in a highly technological society—or maybe because of it—we yearn to connect with others. We want to be together, and to share the koinonia that Jesus died to give us. He designed the home to be a picture of heaven, with members of the family living together in peace and harmony.

Like the members of a church, a family also acts as a body. God has given each member gifts and talents. When they function cooperatively, complementing each other, they accomplish together as a body what the individual parts cannot. It is also true that when one member suffers—as when one part of your body is injured—the entire family suffers.

How effectively we use our homes depends upon our walk with God. The mature woman's house is decorated and ready for dwelling—and sharing. Ideally, each family member knows Jesus Christ personally, and the Holy Spirit is welcome to fill each vessel for ministry. If this is true of you and your home, get ready to experience the most rewarding years of your life.

A Haven for the Heart

Before womankind joined the work force, her supreme role was that of making a home for her family. Today, regardless of the fact that she may be CEO of a major corporation or socially and politically connected, her true identity still comes forth best in her home.

The home is the visual extension of a woman. Here she has created a nest—a place of love, dreams, growth, and security. She has collected treasures along with the things needed for the comfort of her family. She has made a few mistakes—in decorating and otherwise—and is the wiser for them. Having learned the transience of life, she realizes the importance of continuity, the true treasures that are more often intangible than tangible.

The family unit may have changed—children grow up and move away, a spouse dies, an elderly relative moves in—but the essence of the home remains a place of sanctuary for those who dwell here. With her house in order—both physically and spiritually—the mature woman sees beyond the external to the eternal. She discerns truth from counterfeit, the genuine from the fake. With more time for reflection in her home, she is aware that this discernment for the authentic is a product of focusing her eyes on her spiritual Husband. She is actually becoming more and more like Him as she spends time with Him. In the same way a pale etching decorates a plain wall and enlivens a room with subtle hues, the textures and fabrics of a woman's natural life, blended with the supernatural, reflect a masterpiece that is fearfully and wonderfully made.

As she moves through her house, examining each room closely, she will want her home to reflect the inner person she has become. She will want to add touches of the divine—accessories for the soul. These might be devotional books placed in strategic locations, a piece of art featuring some biblical scene or story, lovely framed calligraphy highlighting a Scripture verse that has been especially meaningful in a difficult time, or an open Bible placed on an antique stand. These touches can alter the ambiance of a room and bring the light of the eternal into the commonplace activities of life.

The Bible continually exhorts us to "rest in the Lord," "wait on the Lord," and to "be still and know" that He is God. Therefore, it is important to create places of quiet reflection for all who live in your home. This could be a window nook overlooking a garden or an alcove, created by using a folding screen. It could even be as simple as the corner of a bedroom, my own cozy "pocket of peace" in our mountain house. Here I enjoy a club chair with ottoman, where I prop up my feet, meditate, and reflect on all that the Lord is currently teaching me.

As a woman communes with God more and more, her garden begins to center around her interior life, and her family and home reflect the fruit.

Neighboring

Heirloom: *"They helped every one his neighbor; and every one said to his brother, Be of good courage."*

—Isaiah 41:6 (KJV)

Have you ever suspected that the Lord planted you in the very house and neighborhood in which you reside? Oh, you may have thought it was all your own idea. You may have inherited the family estate or settled in this particular neighborhood for economic reasons or with safety precautions in mind. But in the vocabulary of the Christian woman, there is no such thing as coincidence.

You may be living here because you are the lone "light" on your street or in your community.

In my design business, I deal with lighting—both interior and exterior. Some houses are "day houses" while others are "night houses." Rooms with large expanses of glass and marvelous exterior views qualify as "day houses." At night these large glassed-in areas become black "holes" and artificial lighting is needed to soften the darkness.

The houses I call "night houses" are those with strong color and art. These rooms take on new life at night when lighted properly. Art is enhanced by portrait lights, and directional beams carry the eye to points of interest throughout the house.

Light dispels darkness. Light offers security and protection. Think how welcome you feel when you arrive late at night to find that a lamp has been left on and is still glowing in the window. This message says, "Come in! I care for you. I'm so glad you're home."

For those who live in the home and for neighbors alike, the mature Christian woman is a light, softening the darkness with a message of God's love. She carries it with her everywhere she goes, much like Florence Nightingale did, lifting her lamp to tend the wounded soldiers of the Crimean War. She is the nightlight that offers reassurance. She is the lamp left burning in the window. She is the directional beam, pointing others to the Source of her power.

Ever since Eve, when mankind rejected God's design for intimate fellowship with the Creator, the Lord has waited patiently for each soul to forsake his own selfishness and look again to Him alone. Weary travelers are looking for a way station, a place to be loved and accepted, a light in the window that says, "We're home." Heart-hungry people need to know that "supper is ready." This is our Lord's call to every human heart: *"I love you. I forgive you. Come to the table, for the feast is prepared."*

As they see Christ in you, operating in love and mercy for your family and others, people in your neighborhood will be attracted to your home. They will feel intuitively that compassion will always be available here, that even a stranger could find refuge.

Cooking a lovely meal to welcome newcomers to the neighborhood, taking a cup of coffee or a tall glass of iced tea to the repairman, or arranging flowers for a neighbor returning home from the hospital are all ways of offering refuge to someone who may be caught in one of life's storms.

We can use our porches and decks, our gardens, our living spaces, our bedrooms, and our eating places as potential harbors. But leave the Light on so that your neighbors can find their way through the darkness.

The Gift of Hospitality

A woman who opens her home to others must be mature—whole. God's peace is the Hebrew word *shalom*, which means "wholeness." The whole woman will live at peace in her home. Only then can it become a place of peace for others.

Hospitality is the extension of grace and welcome. The root of the word *hospitality* is "hospital." It's a unique ministry to care for and nurture to health a soul who comes for relief. On a deep level, hospitality may well be akin to doctoring.

When a woman loves God with all of her heart and loves others as herself, every day is "open house." She honors her friends with parties and invites guests for tea. All who enter and partake of the fruit of love, joy, peace, patience, kindness, gentleness, and self-control sense the presence of the Spirit. Offering these blessings to others is an expression of being created in the image of God.

A well-appointed guest room is a beautiful way of saying, "I have a place for you. Come. Eat, rest, and enjoy yourself in my home, which I share with you." A guest room should be equipped with everything a person would need to feel loved—lots of plump pillows on the bed, warm comforters and throws, soft towels for the bath, and a Bible on the bedside table. Touches of your own individual creativity can provide an atmosphere of warmth and invite your guest to draw closer to you and to God.

My mother frames the picture of an expected guest and leaves it on a table in her guest room as a silent gesture of welcome. If a picture is not available, write a note and place it on the pillow for your guest to read before bedtime, or leave a Bible open to a marked passage that will bring blessing.

A friend of mine has set aside a bedroom with its own private entrance and kitchen in a wing that is remote from the rest of the house. This room is used by visiting pastors and church leaders when in need of privacy and rest. Many a saint has found himself renewed in this sanctuary.

Entertaining friends in your home is an expression of love. Food and party preparations allow the hostess and her guests to work together and discover new areas of mutual enjoyment and common interests. An amazing thing happens at such times. When hearts and homes are prepared for friends to come together, a new depth of communication is possible. The gathering can be casual and fun, or profound and deep. A dying to selfish agendas and a preparation to hear the Spirit enriches our communion. Whether enjoying a meal with Oreo cookies and a glass of milk or celebrating a sumptuous feast, the hearts of the hostess and her guests unite, bonding them for future growth together.

We are encouraged in the Scriptures to reach out and bring others into our lives. We are told that there is a blessing when we entertain. The blessing is often the beauty of friendship and an invitation to participate in the lives of others. Giving begets giving, healing of relationships takes place, and friends are drawn to the hospitable home.

Entertaining Angels

Heirloom: *"Don't forget to be kind
to strangers, for some who
have done this have entertained
angels without realizing it!"*

—Hebrews 13:2

Much of life is a mystery. We cannot understand why some things happen as they do and why some people enter our lives. All we can do is trust God with the unknowns—and thank Him for orchestrating them.

Those who trust in the Lord will be strengthened in supernatural ways. In our weakness, He is strong. In our need, He provides. In our distress, He sends relief. I'm absolutely convinced that He has dispatched ministering angels just when I was the most desperate. Sometimes they have looked just like people!

I will never forget a time in late winter when both my daughters and my business were very young. I had not yet married John and was struggling with single motherhood, trying to wear too many hats and juggle too many balls in the air. My mother, sister, and her friend called to tell me they were coming for the weekend to give me some much-needed rest, and I could simply sleep in on Saturday morning as late as I wanted. It sounded fabulous, and I was only too happy to oblige!

While I slept, the three women went out to the front of the house and planted bulbs—dozens of them—then replaced the straw and mulch, leaving no sign of their little secret.

The next spring, I awoke one morning to an amazing sight—tulips, narcissus, and jonquils waking from their winter naps to bloom in a riot of color outside my door. I had no idea how the flowers had gotten there. I certainly hadn't planted them.

But when I questioned my mother, she confessed to the good deed, adding that she and the other two had hoped their gardening scheme would give me the lift I needed. It did much more than that. It taught me that human beings can go on angelic "assignment," planting love in winter soil, to bloom after the cold, dark season is over.

Be on the lookout. You, too, may entertain angels when you least expect it.

Teaching from the Heart

Heirloom: *"You must teach them [the Commandments] to your children and talk about them when you are at home."*

—Deuteronomy 6:7

Home is also the venue for teaching and instruction. Just because your children are all grown up doesn't mean you are exempt from this role. There may be grandchildren, the children of friends, or younger women for whom to model the social graces and the grace of God.

While the wise woman was aware that the child-rearing years would be quickly over and, therefore, invested time and energy in her children in the home, circumstances may have prevented her from being all she could be to them. If this is your story, take advantage of the second chance provided by the mature years. Now perhaps you can be more available as you journey through adulthood with your grown children and can spend quality time with your grandchildren. Grandmothering is a marvelous calling—a time to bless the generations with your presence and the wisdom of your life experiences.

Allow your home to be a base for all the generations. Open your home to your grandchildren's friends. As they come and go, be alert to every opportunity to impart affirmation and blessing. Be prepared to meet heart needs. The younger generation may have their own lingo and style of dress, but love is a language and a garment all its own and spans all differences.

Home Study

Women have traditionally been a support for each other, and in our post-industrial isolation, many need the security of someone's home in order to share openly and allow themselves to be emotionally vulnerable. As women meet and study together, their needs are met and they grow. They are equipped to be more than conquerors.

The church has its place in ministry, but as the first institution created by God, the home is a natural schoolhouse for the study of His Word. For everyone from the youngest member of a family to the friends who drop by for coffee and to break the "bread of life," the Word is the source of spiritual nourishment. As women meet casually, with all barriers dropped, they are able to relate on a level that is not possible in other settings.

Out of my own heart hunger for the things of God, I began to study His Word in earnest. I was more faithful to Bible studies and worship services in our church. But I found an unexpected blessing in home Bible studies.

I gravitated toward those homes where the Bible was revered and taught. There I met new friends and mingled with old. As we studied together, I began to see everything differently. Stripped away were old perceptions. Each person took on new value as I saw her through God's eyes. I could appreciate her gifts and talents, her unique preciousness, her own distinctive calling. I could measure her, not by the world's standards, but by God's Word that declares each person "a new creation in Christ."

A friend of mine relates how her own home has been used to bring healing—for herself and for other women.

This friend had rejected her past because of abuse, but she began to see that the Lord was calling her to face her painful background. In this process, a Bible teacher helped her realize that she could use her home to bless women she had known since childhood. They would meet together and feel comfortable. She envisioned her house with light, airy colors—symbolic of freedom and release—especially in the family room where the women would be gathering.

Five years later, recalling the Bible teacher's vision, she began contacting her old friends and inviting them to meet with her to study God's Word. They accepted eagerly. For the past five years, the women have prayed together, studied the Bible together, and shared openly. In being "real"—developing transparency and honesty—old hurts have been healed, and God's Word has brought life to dead places.

🕸

For the mature woman in her own home, time can now be invested in prayer, study, and journaling her thoughts. These disciplines will release a wellspring of life as she continues to grow in knowledge and wisdom.

The home provides privacy and protection for the development of your inner person. Use this time and place to grow deeper in God's Word and His ways. Bask in the refreshing flow of the Spirit. Spiritual maturity comes with practice—practicing His presence.

10

Going Deeper

Heirloom: *"Don't store up treasures here
on earth where they can erode away or
may be stolen. Store them in heaven where
they will never lose their value."*

—Matthew 6:19,20

After years of children and career, long hours and sleepless nights, suddenly it seems there is a little more time—glorious, luxurious time—for yourself. Time to smell the roses. Time to read something besides textbooks or professional journals. Time to explore new frontiers, to take a good, hard look at your personal interior—the inner you.

You have finished your house, or perhaps you have moved to a new location with less space and lower maintenance. You have learned to prioritize, to simplify, to declutter, and to organize your life.

As you go deeper with the Lord, there is a hunger for spiritual truths. I remember the gnawing sensation that was stirred in me when the Holy Spirit began to woo me. I could not get enough revelation of God's Word. Many nights I fell asleep, propped up in bed, with the Bible open on my lap. I was literally covered by the Word.

This period was an intense time of healing and restoration. My desires changed. Now I was more eager to go to a Bible study than to an antique symposium. The principles of God were becoming clearer. I knew that the pathway opening before me was guiding me to freedom and a depth I had never known before.

Bible study and prayer opened a chamber of my heart. As I studied, I began to examine my own interior. It needed much cleansing and redecorating. Very gently and sweetly, God began a correction of my thoughts and actions. He began to replace old furnishings with His priceless heirlooms. I was being remade according to His original design for me, and I knew it.

Going deeper is a process that requires many layers of recovery and revelation. We go from glory to glory until we achieve the fullness of God, that state of being that is not whole and complete—fully mature—until we enter the gates of heaven.

God Calling

Heirloom: *"Very quietly I speak. Listen to My voice. Never heed the voices of the world— only the tender Divine Voice."*

—Two Listeners

The Holy Spirit is the revealer of all truth. A believer does not just suddenly decide she wants to learn more about the things of God and then take a giant leap into the unknown. She is tenderly wooed by the Spirit who whispers to her heart like a lover: "Rise up, my love, my fair one, and come away...." (The Song of Solomon 2:10).

Is He speaking to your heart? Will you go to Him? Will you leave the familiar to embrace the unfamiliar? Or will you remain locked in traditions and trivial pursuits?

When Jesus called to Peter one stormy night while he was fishing, the disciple answered that call by stepping out of the safety and familiarity of his fishing boat and literally walking on water, on his way to the Master. As long as he kept his eyes fixed on Jesus, he was "mysteriously" able to remain on top of the sea. But when he glanced around and realized what was happening, and that the waves were restless and angry, he was terrified and began to sink (see Matthew 14:25-32).

With your eyes on Jesus, you will be able to launch out into the deep. But if you are more concerned about the circumstances around you and allow fear to take hold, you will go under. Going deeper requires determined faith and discipline to hear His voice, followed by obedient action.

God is calling you to abandon completely selfish desires and agendas. He wants to give you so much more. He wants to sharpen your spiritual senses. He wants to teach you deeper lessons of faith and unlock such mysteries as the gifts of the Spirit, the offices of the Spirit, inner healing, physical healing, and prophetic callings. These and more are part of the abundant life in Christ. Once you have accepted His invitation and tasted of this abundant life, you will never want to return to your former ways or beliefs.

One mystery with which I now have first-hand experience is emotional healing. In fact, I am a walking miracle! In the past twenty-five years or so, I have gone from panic attacks to peace, from cowering in my home to appearing on national television! Only God could have brought that kind of inner healing.

In my mid-twenties during my divorce, I experienced fear, which resulted in panic attacks so debilitating that I did not want to get out of bed. I actually thought I was going to die. What a lie! Panic attacks are really demonic attacks, and I was almost persuaded to believe that I would never be any better.

When I began to understand the truth of God's Word, my focus shifted from myself to my Savior. The truth of God showed me clearly that Jesus was in control and was holding me close. He would never leave me alone. As God began to breathe life into me, the healing began.

In my mature years, I now know how to face down the enemy when he comes in attempting to rob, kill, and destroy. Satan is a coward. He has to flee when we resist him. I just cry out, "Jesus!" and that Name that is above all names is sufficient to send the enemy running for cover.

The Secret Place of Prayer

Prayer can be as simple as calling out the name of Jesus in an emergency, or full dialogue—a two-way conversation—with your heavenly Father. As His child, you are invited to join Him in the "secret place" and call Him by His more intimate name, *Abba,* "Daddy."

I will never forget the first time after my father's death when I realized that God had not left me without a "Daddy." I knew that I was welcome to climb into His lap at any time and nestle in His arms, to talk with Him, or simply to listen to His heartbeat. Since He knows my thoughts even before my lips utter a word, sometimes our deepest communion is in silence. I am His daughter, and because I am confident of that relationship, I have not missed my earthly father nearly as much.

I know God sees every detail of my life and that He has numbered every hair of my head. I can tell Him during the day everything that concerns me, and know that He cares. Then I listen for His answers to my questions and to His instructions. This kind of interaction produces an ongoing communion that translates into strength for the journey and peace in the midst of the storm.

The intimate one-on-One kind of prayer is essential to going deeper with the Lord. In her book, *Power of the Secret Place,* Bobbie Jean Merck writes:

> It is not what is done behind the pulpit, in front of it, in the work place, or in the home that determines your God, but rather what is done in the secret place.
>
> What we do in our secret place reveals who and what our god is. If I just seek time to relax or indulge in some preoccupation, then that becomes my god. If I seek time to be with the Almighty God, to worship Him, and have fellowship with Him, then He is my God.

If we do not spend quality time alone with God, we will not know His voice when He speaks in a crowd. We must guard these times of intimacy well. It is here, in the secret place, that we can speak in our own special language of love to the One who cherishes us most of all.

When I was younger, I didn't understand the significance of being a woman of prayer. I was so busy caring for my family and running my business that every minute was filled to capacity. As I have matured, God has taught me the practical benefits of prayer. He has shown me that if I will take care of His business, He will take care of mine.

I ask Him for help in resolving some situation with a difficult client and—zap—it's done! I ask Him for direction in making important decisions, and He opens doors and puts the right people in my path. He is my Partner in every aspect of my life.

Prayer Partners

He also leads us to prayer partners in the flesh. When I was making one of the most important decisions of my life, remarriage, the Lord gave me clarity—and He gave me John. I knew with a deep inner knowing that this man was God's gift to me.

On our honeymoon, realizing the power of two coming together in agreement, we prayed together as we fell asleep. Holding hands, I felt the covering of John's love, and a huge weight lifted from my shoulders. But it was prayer that cemented our union. Realizing that God is our Foundation gives our marriage stability and strength. We are grounded in Him, individually and as a couple.

I have had other prayer partners throughout my life. Some have mentored me. Others have been in my life for a season. Now, as a mature woman, I have invited four friends into my life as accountability partners. We pray together frequently, and they have my permission to point out anything that might need correction or clarification. Needless to say, they never offer a word of instruction unless they have first prayed about it long and hard. I know they love me, have my welfare at heart, and desire only that my life and ministry glorify God. Therefore, I can receive from them. In this relationship is great comfort and reassurance that undergirds my deeper walk with God.

&e

As we go deeper with the Lord, we will learn something about intercession—standing in the gap for someone through prayer. We mean well when we so glibly say, "I'll be praying for you." But true intercession is best done in the secret place and comes after much prayer and groaning in the Spirit. It is a powerful weapon for breaking strongholds in lives and calling forth those things God wants to accomplish. It is wise for a mature woman, acting as His ambassador, to surround herself with strong intercessors. God has promised that if we "dwell" here—reside, stay fixed, remain—we shall be living "under the shadow of the Almighty," within His protective covering.

Studying God's Word

The Word of God is life. It is the voice of our Creator speaking to sustain and nurture that life. It is the pathway of peace. It is the North Star by which we chart our course through this world. In God's Word there are solutions to every problem, a provision for every need. In His Word, there is power to change hearts and transform lives to conform to His will.

Studying the Word of God becomes amplified as the Spirit takes believers deeper. As we study precept upon precept, we are alerted to subtle meanings. Passages leap off the pages with new life.

Paul says it best:

> When I first came to you...my preaching was very plain, not with a lot of oratory and human wisdom, but the Holy Spirit's power was in my words, proving to those who heard them that the message was from God. I did this because I

wanted your faith to stand firmly upon God, not on man's great ideas.

Yet when I am among *mature* Christians I do speak with words of great wisdom, but not the kind that comes from here on earth, and not the kind that appeals to the great men of this world, who are doomed to fall. Our words are wise because they are from God, telling of God's wise plan to bring us into the glories of heaven. This plan was *hidden* in former times, though it was made for our benefit before the world began....

That is what is meant by the Scriptures which say that no mere man has ever seen, heard or even imagined what wonderful things God has ready for those who love the Lord. But we know about these things because God has sent his Spirit to tell us, and his Spirit searches out and shows us all of God's deepest secrets.

1 Corinthians 2:1,4-6,7,9,10

Through the Spirit who reveals the meaning of God's Word, we are finally able to understand many of the principles that have always seemed so mysterious. *We get it!*

Opening the Windows of Heaven

Heirloom: *"Bring all the tithes into the storehouse....if you do, I will open up the windows of heaven for you and pour out a blessing so great you won't have room enough to take it in!"*

—Malachi 3:10

Giving is one of God's mysteries that becomes clearer as we take Him at His word and begin to practice it. With the command to give—of our time, talents, and financial assets—we receive an incredible promise. "If you give, you will get! Your gift will return to you in full and overflowing measure, pressed down, shaken together to make room for more, and running over. Whatever measure you use to give— large or small—will be used to measure what is given back to you" (Luke 6:38).

Do you get the picture? Although I don't do as much cooking now as I used to do, I can still see a homemaker in her kitchen, measuring out brown sugar for a recipe. She presses the sugar into the measuring cup so that there will be "room for more," until it spills over. God's gifts to us are just like that cup—overflowing with His bounty.

As younger women, we may have seen our cup as half-empty rather than half-full. Maturity—and the anointing of the Holy Spirit—shows us the true picture. God is a lavish Giver. He loves to give good gifts to His children, and when we give generously, He is delighted to return the gift with interest.

I learned more of how this principle works about twelve years ago. On a hot July evening in Atlanta, I attended a Bible study, where a lovely lady had a prophetic word for me.

"God has a work for you to do in Chattanooga, Tennessee," she said. "When the call comes, you will know that it is from God, and you will do whatever you are asked to do."

Two months later a telephone call came from a friend's client, Judy, who works with Precept Ministries, the internationally-known inductive Bible study ministry founded by Kay Arthur. Judy was in town doing research on interior design for a new building that was being built by the ministry in Chattanooga. Upon hearing her request, my friend had referred Judy to me for help in locating the items needed.

I met with Judy a few hours later in my office. As she opened the blueprint for the building and rolled it out on my work table, I saw in the architectural scale box the name, "The Grace Kinser Memorial Building." I gasped. *John and I lived in Mrs. Kinser's last home!* This was no coincidence, no random meeting. This was a divine appointment.

A few weeks later I met Kay Arthur herself. What a precious saint she is! It was pure joy to assist in selecting colors, furnishings, fabrics, and carpet for the new building.

When the project was completed, I did not accept any compensation for my services. Since Kay and I have the same Father, I was only too happy to offer my gifts and talents to help my sister in Christ.

My offering was multiplied back to me in so many ways—"in full and overflowing measure." The immediate blessing was in getting to know Kay and being allowed to sow seed into a ministry that has been used around the world to bring the Word of God to every tribe and every nation. Most recently—eleven years after we concluded the decorating project—Kay introduced me to Harvest House Publishers. God's blessings have come full circle.

Spiritual Warfare

Heirloom: *"Enemy-occupied territory—*
that is what this world is. Christianity is
the story of how the rightful king has
landed...and is calling us all to take part
in a great campaign of sabotage."

—C. S. Lewis

When we are involved in kingdom work, we are fair game for harrassment and attack in the spiritual realm. Before I began my deeper walk with God, I was completely ignorant of the fact that we, as Christians, are engaged in a war. I was enjoying a stroll in the park while more seasoned warriors were doing hand-to-hand combat with the enemy of our souls—Satan.

"Onward, Christian Soldiers" was merely an old hymn, one that is sung seldom, if ever, anymore. But I was uniniti-ated in such matters. For one thing, I hadn't the faintest notion of what soldiers do—other than the fact that they look wonderful in their uniforms, march in parades, and fight in wartime. Well-bred Southern ladies are taught, from birth, to look for the positive aspects of any situation, to maintain one's composure, and to be polite in any event. Hardly the substance of soldiering.

When I discovered that I must regroup and retrain, I asked my husband to tell me something about war. As John talked, I took notes, scribbling frantically:

"War is a science," he began. "First of all, an army never goes into battle without being fully informed about the enemy they will engage. What is the nature of the enemy? What kinds of tactics are likely to be used? What kinds of battle strategies have been employed in past confrontations?

"Next, an army must be armed and prepared—both offensively and defensively. Keeping in mind the possible strategies that may be used, training begins and weapons are issued.

"Plans call for strikes and counteroffensives to be devised and coordinated. In training, soldiers are drilled until they can react instantaneously and without forethought.

"An army cannot function without provisions. Food, fuel, and ammunition must be carried to the battlefield, and extra supplies and reinforcements ready for delivery."

John paused, looking off into space as he thought. "But above all," he concluded, "an army doesn't go into battle without being determined to win."

Immediately I could see parallels for spiritual warfare. I learned more about the face of our enemy as I searched the Scriptures for everything I could find on Satan, Lucifer, the father of lies, the "prince of darkness."

He is devious and cunning. He is out to rob, kill, and destroy. He is often disguised as an angel of light. It gets worse:

> We are not fighting against people made of flesh and blood, but against persons without bodies—the evil rulers of the unseen world, those mighty satanic beings and great evil princes of darkness who rule this world; and against huge numbers of wicked spirits in the spirit world.
>
> —Ephesians 6:12

But the more I read, the more excited I became. God has not left us without a plan, advice about preparation for battle, and provisions—"the full armor of God"—that is able to help us overtake and defeat our enemy.

> Use every piece of God's armor to resist the enemy whenever he attacks, and when it is all

over, you will still be standing up. But to do this, you will need the strong belt of truth and the breastplate of God's approval. Wear shoes that are able to speed you on as you preach the Good News of peace with God. In every battle you will need faith as your shield to stop the fiery arrows aimed at you by Satan. And you will need the helmet of salvation and the sword of the Spirit— which is the Word of God.

Pray all the time. Ask God for anything in line with the Holy Spirit's wishes. Plead with him, reminding him of your needs, and keep praying earnestly for all Christians everywhere.

—verses 13-18

Be on guard. Sometimes the enemy launches surprise attacks. The strongest ones may come from within the family. When you are aware of the enemy's strategies, you can see the plan for division—mother against daughter, father against son. It is sad when families are separated; it may take generations to restore fellowship.

Every day, as we prepare to face the next twenty-four hours with its inevitable skirmishes with the enemy, we must put on the whole armor of God, not leaving out one single item that is designed for our safety and protection. Then we can step out into our world, eyes fixed on our Commander, confident of victory!

Saving Souls

I am so thrilled to be a mature woman of faith living in this day. The trumpet is blowing, and women are responding. God is raising up an army of women who are teaching, preaching, praying, and breaking through to a lost and dying world.

We are a global society with instant access to all people everywhere. As a child, I can recall putting my quarter for foreign missions in the collection plate at Christmas. Today our children are in Internet chat rooms, communicating directly with people from all over the world! There are reports of conversions by computer, prayer requests made and answered, and missionaries reporting on conditions in the most remote corners of the earth.

Women are moving to the forefront in ministry. From ancient Bible days to the present, we have always been busy about our Father's business. Kay Arthur, Beverly LaHaye, Marilyn Hickey, and many others are examples of contemporary warrior women, marching for Jesus into corporate boardrooms, inner city ghettos, and upscale gated communities.

The mature woman is available to the Lord for whatever He calls her to do, wherever He leads. She is directing Bible studies, interceding, ministering in prisons, and hosting prayer meetings in her home.

She is aware that revival is breaking out all over the world—in Argentina, Africa, India, China, Russia, and in remote jungle villages not identified on any map. Mature people who have time to travel can participate in praying forth the revival and bringing it in.

In our "retirement" years, John and I have been privileged to visit many countries and continents. We collect so much more than souvenirs of memorable trips; we collect souls. John makes it a point never to leave a place without leading someone, targeted by the Holy Spirit, to the Lord.

On a trip to Portugal, we met a versatile young man, Ricardo, who wore many hats at the estate where we stayed: driver, overseer, and tour guide.

Upon helping us plan our stay, he suggested we include a visit to Fatima, a site considered to be a place of miracles.

A beautiful cathedral is built on the grounds where millions come to pray.

As we entered the church, Ricardo excused himself and went to the front to kneel and pray at the altar. Being of another faith, John and I stayed at the back, praying quietly in the pews.

As we were leaving, Ricardo told us that he had been praying for some personal needs, and John felt led to share his personal testimony of receiving Christ as his Savior.

Ricardo seemed moved, and John pressed in. "Would you like to join me in prayer to receive Jesus?"

"You would do that for me?"

"I certainly would." John put his hand on the young man's shoulder and asked him to repeat after him: "Dear Jesus, have mercy on my lost soul and forgive my sins. Take away this heavy load, this awful burden, from my heart and set me free. Deliver me from every wrong desire and every bad habit that binds my life, and dear Lord give me your peace for my soul, and your power to make me a child right now.

"Dear Lord, I receive you into my heart this very moment as my Lord and Savior. I will serve you from this hour, all the days of my life. This I will do by the help of God and in the name of Jesus Christ. Amen."

Ricardo's face was shining at the end of the prayer. "Oh, something happen to me!" he said. "Something warm here." He put his hand over his heart. "I have prayed here many times but never have I felt this way."

John smiled. "This is a place of miracles, isn't it? You are born anew."

Together with two other friends from our group, we lit candles in celebration of Ricardo's new birth.

The things of the material world no longer dazzle as they once did. I am depositing treasures in heaven. That heavenly deposit, along with the loved ones who have gone before, are loosening my hold on earth.

❧

Heirloom: *There is awesome power in women. God has chosen women to serve as the vehicles through which entry is made into this world. And He has shared His creativity with women.*
—T.D. Jakes

The
Well-Seasoned
Woman

11

In Full Bloom

✓ Heirloom: *"Think of a rose, and you
won't mind the thorns—
They're a part of the miracle, too."*[2]

—B. J. Hoff

When John and I built our first home, we included
plans for a formal rose garden. We planted over 250 rose-
bushes that supplied us with an abundance of beauty and
fragrance all during the season. Watching the roses bloom in
the garden, I have always felt a certain magical expectation.
With each day, a blossoming rose moves a little closer to its
destiny.

As a woman over fifty, I can think of no better metaphor
for the feminine experience than the opening of a rose blossom. A mature woman is a rose in full bloom. Nothing compares with the beauty of this flower when it has reached its
fullest potential, and nothing in the life of the maturing
woman approaches her beauty as she grows up more fully in
Christ. The way the petals seem to reach for the sun reminds
me of my own journey toward intimacy with God. With each

day I struggle to reach beyond myself, and in doing so, discover my true potential for love, happiness, peace, and service.

A rosebud represents the youth of a rose. The heart of the bud holds the warmth of the flower, but we will not see the rose reach maturity until it opens. Heat from the sun will cause the bud to blossom and slowly the petals will begin to unfurl. It is at this point that the fragrance of the rose is freed to waft on the air.

In the bud stage, it is impossible to tell what the rose will look like. The warm, darker coloring of the bud will cool to reveal the color of the full bloom. It is only when the rose is in full bloom that we can see at last the beauty the bud has kept secretly locked away.

The rose is fully matured in a matter of days—a process that takes us years to achieve. Women who have blossomed into their full maturity bear the beauty and fragrance of a life "hidden in Christ."

But roses also bear thorns, and sometimes the petals of the flower are torn by the plant's own thorns—or those of another. Saints of God are called to endure pain as they struggle toward maturity. Think of the great women of faith who suffered along the path of their destiny in God. Corrie ten Boom, Joni Eareckson Tada, Catherine Marshall, and so many others. The life of mature beauty is not without the price of pain.

The Soil of Gratitude

The roots of a woman in full bloom are planted in a grateful heart. God tells us in His Word to rejoice in Him, to give thanks in all things, and to find our complete satisfaction in Him. Because of this close relationship with her Creator, the heart of a woman of faith is full of gratitude.

The spiritually mature woman knows that her efforts are futile without Jesus, that she does nothing of eternal significance without His power. However, in the strength of the Lord, she can do all things (see Philippians 4:13). God progressively teaches her to lay down her own agenda and take up His. As she dies to her flesh, she is amazed at how He takes her to new and higher places than she ever dreamed possible. Things that have perplexed her for years are cleared away, and she finds completion and fulfillment. For this abundant life, she gives praise to the Lord.

True praise and worship is nothing more than the overflow of grateful hearts. God dwells in the midst of praise, and we are ushered into His presence through gifted worship leaders. I am learning, as a mature woman, to appreciate the diversity of musical gifts in the body of Christ. In our church, with a membership of approximately ten thousand, we are occasionally blessed with visiting musicians, many from the contemporary Christian culture. Such people as Michael W. Smith, Babbie Mason, and Twila Paris directly influence the younger generation. As mature women whose musical tastes may run to the classical more than the contemporary, we can stand by with affirmation, encouragement, and gratitude for these young musicians who are affecting an entire generation who need to hear the message in their own "language."

Gratitude begets gratitude, and people are drawn to the mature woman and her God. Out of her intimacy with Him, she develops a strength that is reflected in everything she does. She is calm and serene in the midst of calamity. She is generous in time of need. Others are blessed by talking with her; their spirits are lifted at the sound of her voice. The presence of the Holy Spirit within her penetrates the dark corners of their lives as they encounter the light.

A friend who was dying of cancer asked for me. Although her family had gathered, it appeared that no one quite understood what she needed or how to comfort her. Her husband, who had waited on her faithfully throughout her illness, was eager to help. He stood by, wringing his hands. "Honey, can I get you some more pillows, a blanket?"

What she needed was not another blanket but a covering of prayer. I stepped forward, took her hand, and looked deep into her eyes. Then I prayed for her, a simple prayer of release. She needed someone who knew when to be quiet and when to speak, when to fight for her life and when to let go and let God claim His own. She calmed down immediately, feeling His peace and grateful for His comforting touch at the end of her struggle.

Women bloom best in the fertile soil of gratitude. Cultivate that characteristic in your prayer life. Ask God to give you a grateful heart and then thank Him when He supplies your need.

The Water of the Word

Heirloom: *"Jesus replied....The water
I give...becomes a perpetual spring
within them, watering them
forever with eternal life.'"*

—John 4:13,14

The spiritually mature woman knows who she is in Christ Jesus. She ventures boldly into the throne room of God, believing that, like Queen Esther, her Creator has called her for such a time as this. She hears His instructions through the daily refreshing of the Word and knows that pleasing Him is her true life's mission.

As she has matured, she has learned that fear of man is a snare that prevents her from enjoying God's pleasure. Therefore, in order not to miss His life in all its abundance, she takes God at His Word and is bold as a lion, even if her demeanor is quiet and feminine.

She seeks God's approval moment by moment. As a parent often instructs a child with a look, so a child of God—even at age sixty, seventy, or eighty—beholds Him with spiritual eyes and looks to His Word for guidance and correction throughout the day.

The Scriptures assure her that He will provide in the event of death and disaster. He has taught her that He will never leave her nor forsake her, and that He will strengthen her in her weakness. Because she has learned well, through time and testing, others are inspired to ask how she can remain steady in such a turbulent world. Her answer lies in her living testimony and she bears witness, often without a word. Instinctively, some recognize the God-ness in her and desire Him for themselves.

So much of who she is resides in the Word of God—the Living Word and the written Word. Corrie ten Boom knew the power of God's Word. When being inducted into the concentration camp where her sister Betsie was later to die, Corrie managed to smuggle in a Bible under her clothing. Despite the security measures taken in that camp, including strip searches of all incoming prisoners, God "blinded" the eyes of the guard, and Corrie and Betsie were able to bring the Word into that camp.

Late at night, when they were supposed to be sleeping, Corrie read aloud—first, only in devotional times with Betsie; later, to thirsty prisoners who begged for a sip of this "water of life." Truly, the Word was life to them, easing the agony of their imprisonment and setting fellow captives free as they heard the Word and gladly surrendered their lives to the Author.

Whether inside the walls of a prison camp or liberated, the souls of these poor prisoners were continually watered by the Word until it became a "perpetual spring within them, watering them forever with eternal life."

Living Water

Life with no boundaries parallel stagnant waters. A swamp or pond where the water is not flowing breeds death—so, too, the life without the borders of the authority of God's Word. This kind of stagnation is easy to see in the life of a drug addict who is controlled by the need for drugs. What may not be as apparent is the woman who has become stagnant in her relationships—with her heavenly Father, family members, or friends.

When Jesus asked the woman at the well for a drink of water, her life was a virtual swamp. She had had five husbands and a miserable reputation. As He gave her His living water—the life of the Spirit—she moved beyond the borders of her own small existence and ran to tell the neighbors about this man who knew everything about her. The Living Water cleansed her, bubbled up, and spilled over into the lives of everyone she met. Her life became the stream of God's grace that connected with the river of her community and, ultimately, far beyond the borders of the village to the great ocean of society.

As the river of life rises in a person's heart, the prophet Jeremiah describes the water as covering toes, then ankles, knees, hips, waist, and finally lifting that individual to float along with the strong currents and rapids. A life immersed in the Holy Spirit is buoyant and free! The woman saturated with the love of God rests in the knowledge that the Water of Life is wide and deep and that her commission is to all the world. She will desire to reach beyond her own immediate circumstances to embrace the nations and offer them a drink of this Living Water so they will never thirst again.

The Light of the Son

Heirloom: *"I am the Light of the world. So if you follow me, you won't be stumbling through the darkness, for living light will flood your path."*

—John 8:12

The woman in full bloom has recklessly abandoned herself to Jesus and offered everything in her life for His use—her body, her mind, her talents, and her home. This exchanged life allows her to be filled with the Presence of the Lord and for the gifts of the Spirit to operate in timely sequence.

Her greatest delight is in being with Jesus and in learning of His Kingdom. She has emptied herself of performance for the sake of acceptance by the world and is now ready to move out in God's will. Filled with His Spirit, she is able to defy the enemy of her soul and to leap over all obstacles.

Because her relationship with Jesus has been so intimate, she trusts Him with the tiniest details of her heart as well as the huge hurdles in life. Trusting in God has become a fantastic adventure for her, and although her physical and mental condition may be weakening, her inner person is growing stronger and stronger.

Mature women don't have to stumble in the dark as they grow older. The light of Christ floods their path and illuminates all that He has yet for them to do. Although in their latter years, these women are forming an army that is rising up for active service. Despite the infirmities of age, they have no intention of shutting down. Just walk into nursing homes and assisted care facilities, and you will find women at the height of their ministry—leading Bible studies, praying with fellow residents, mentoring those who are younger in the faith. They have achieved senior status and are realizing their fullest potential.

The Promise of Pruning

My husband's love of rose gardening is a hobby he shared with his father. John has taught me a lot about roses, and in the process, much about life as well. It is necessary, he tells me, to prune the bushes so that the new growth will bear superior blooms.

For the greatest results, pruning takes place in stages. Pruning—"to cut off or cut back for better shape or more fruitful growth"—should begin in the early spring. In the summer, after the bush has completed its cycle, we cut away what is left of the bloom in order for renewal to begin again. Finally, in the autumn months, a third pruning prepares the bush for winter dormancy.

The rosebush, much like a woman's heart, requires almost daily care and maintenance. Pruning the bush ensures not only its survival but its productivity as well. The old growth takes energy and vital sustenance from the root of the plant. No rose can achieve its fullest beauty if, during the season of blooming, it has to fight for its very survival. This painful pruning is necessary to produce beauty in abundance. It is part of the process. Just as in our inner rose gardens, where the more roses we cut, the more roses are produced.

As Roy Lessin says in his lovely little devotional book, *A Fruitful Life:* "When God prunes you, He is saying 'I love you too much to allow what is harmful to continue in your life.' Pruning purifies you, strengthens your character, and brings glory to His name. When God says no to you, He is only saying yes to something higher and better."

The mature woman has endured her seasons of pruning. She has felt the Gardener's shears, cutting away the unnecessary, the trivial. She recognizes the importance of being shaped so that she is able to bear the fruit that will draw others to God.

If the rose in full bloom holds the true beauty of the plant, this is true for the maturing woman. Her essence is a combination of experience, grace, confidence, wisdom, and freedom. Her life, rooted and grounded in faith and pruned of harmful habits and lifestyle patterns, produces magnificent fruit—love, joy, peace, patience, kindness, goodness, faithfulness, gentleness, and self-control—evidence of the Spirit living in her.

Every woman who desires to bloom must submit herself to the Gardener of her soul, who will tenderly nurture and tend her, but will use the shears when necessary.

In Full Bloom

A woman in full bloom knows that she has received her very life from God and that she has been designed to give as she has received. She follows the lead of the One who gave His only Son to die for her. In turn, our Father asks us to give unconditionally and generously.

This woman tests her motives constantly to make sure her heart is sincere. Why is she living at this time? What is her purpose? To please herself, other women, the men in her life, or God? Does she invite to her home only those who can reciprocate, or to fulfill her "social obligations"? Or does she obey that clear Word of God that instructs:

> "When you put on a dinner...don't invite friends, brothers, relatives, and rich neighbors! For they will return the invitation. Instead, invite the poor, the crippled, the lame, and the blind. Then at the resurrection of the godly, God will reward you for inviting those who can't repay you."
>
> —Luke 14:12-14

As the mature woman lives and gives with no thought of receiving in return, she grows toward her destiny as a daughter of the King.

Ruth, the young Moabite widow, gave up everything she had known—homeland, friends, and family—to accompany her mother-in-law, Naomi, back to Bethlehem. As this young woman with a great servant heart followed her dead husband's mother to a strange land, she went not knowing what lay in store for her. She was simply prepared to live the rest of her life caring for the needs of her aging mother-in-law.

But God had much more for her. A wealthy relative of the family, Boaz, seeing their destitution, purchased Ruth as his wife, according to the custom of the day. What a blessing! At that moment Ruth could not know that from her womb would come the lineage of King David, and that she would be in the line of Jesus Himself, our true Kinsman-Redeemer. We cannot out-give God!

❧

In the early 1970s, a sudden snowstorm blew through South Carolina, leaving eight inches of snow in its wake. Since it rarely snows in Charleston, the schools closed early, and the grocery stores were jammed with shoppers, their carts piled high with food.

My parents, who lived in Orangeburg sixty-eight miles from my sister and me, were in Charleston at the time and called us to come home. But the snow fell so quickly that travel became hazardous, and we decided to wait out the blizzard in the city with good friends.

On the Interstate and side roads, people were soon stranded in the bitter cold. With traffic at a standstill, the National Guard sent helicopters to rescue the unfortunate travelers and place them in motels or private homes that would take them in.

My family home, located about four miles from Interstate 26, was one of the first to which the Guard turned for help. Seeing a helicopter land on the front lawn at "Willbrook" and strangers stepping off to trudge through the snow, my parents rushed out to greet them with open arms and warm Southern hospitality.

"Senator, these people were stranded out on I-26," the guardsman explained, "and we're placin' them with nice folks like yourself and Miss Margaret. I told them that, if I didn't miss my guess, they'd be apt to have the time of their lives," he added with a wink.

Before long, all six bedrooms were filled. The eight visitors were thankful to be out of the storm, and my parents set out to make them feel right at home.

Mother quickly got to know everybody and discovered that two of the women were hair stylists and that all of them knew how to play bridge. It wasn't long before all the ladies had makeovers, with lively bridge games going on in the living room and family room.

The group bonded beautifully. Everyone had a turn in the kitchen, helping my mother with the meals. Unlike Charlestonians, who had been able to get to the grocery stores before the storm hit with its full intensity, my parents were dependent upon what they had stored in the freezer. My mother later told me that she cooked up everything in both freezers and was so glad to have a reason to clean them out.

It took nearly a week before the snow melted, and when it came time for the guests to leave, they all cried. The loving way in which my parents had reached out to eight complete strangers had made them family. Mother still hears from her "Northern adopted relatives," who will never forget the storm of '72.

In my mother's mature years, she has come to the full knowledge of who she is and how the Lord wants to use her home. She saw the storm not as an imposition, but as an opportunity to serve. Since she was relying on the Lord, she could welcome strangers in a snowstorm and clean out her freezer in the process.

The mature woman can laugh at the future because she knows life is full of serendipity and surprises. The heart that is restful is open to play. Only when one is truly relaxed can moments of hilarity take place. The stranded strangers, doing makeovers and playing bridge, exhibit an enforced rest and recreation. But it was their serene hostess who set the pace.

Mother also invested her resources, both spiritually and materially, and her investments grew with interest. As in the parables, the "bread" multiplied and needs were met. When her guests commented on the delicious "turkey" sandwiches, Miss Margaret explained that the "turkey" was really pheasant from the bottom of the freezer. Her guests wept as they left because they had received such royal treatment and because they had experienced the delight of community. For that brief span of time, the senator's home became the base for healing, and eternity broke into life in the low country of South Carolina.

Serving is another form of giving. Once a woman has surrendered to God's will, her home base is a magnificent medium for serving others. Offering a meal, a cup of coffee, a party, a resting place, or simply a listening ear, the woman in full bloom moves in serenity, seizing each moment to plant seeds of God's love and grace in the lives of people she meets.

🌺

At sunset, our rose gardens were spectacular. The warm glow of the setting sun bathed the blossoms in a wash of peach and purple. Here in this setting we often held late-afternoon suppers with special friends, using baskets of roses to adorn the tables. We also hosted weddings here, the fabulous display of fragrant blooms the only decoration needed.

As the sun begins its descent in our lives, we are able to see a whole new world of beauty before us. The setting has become more ethereal; the atmosphere, more heavily perfumed with the scent of godliness and grace. We are just moving into a new place of usefulness, never dreamed of nor anticipated. Truly, the best is before us, just waiting over the horizon.

12

Mentoring

Heirloom: *"A teacher affects eternity; he can never tell where his influence stops."*

—Henry Brooks Adams

Just as Miss Margaret modeled Southern hospitality and the love of God before her unexpected guests, so all mature women of faith can model spiritual gifts and graces. These women fill the role of mentor.

A mentor is a wise and trusted friend, teacher, and counselor. Even the woman who has no children of her own can bless us by passing on the treasures of truth she has learned. With the voice of wisdom, she gives advice and offers insight and direction. Mentors are gifts of God's love, the bearers of truth and life for those they teach.

Refinement, elegance, and grace, as well as experience and factual information, are fully developed in the mature woman; therefore, she has much to offer others, and her life is filled with purpose as long as she lives. I remember marveling at my grandmother when we shared time together on lazy Sunday afternoons. A lifetime of experience had equipped her with intuition and insight. Everything she had to say was validated by the wisdom obtained through her personal pilgrimage. And so I listened—and learned.

One of the greatest examples of this powerful gift of teaching is the relationship that existed between Helen Keller and her tutor and companion, Anne Sullivan. Anne brought peace into Helen's dark world. To this child, rendered blind, deaf, and dumb by a severe illness, the woman offered the gifts of love, compassion, patience, and the empowering strength of language. Language was like light itself to young Helen.

"The mystery of language was revealed to me," she wrote. "I knew that 'w-a-t-e-r' meant the wonderful cool something that was flowing over my hand. That living world awakened my soul, gave it light, joy, set it free!" Such is the power of mentoring.

My Mentors

In addition to my grandmothers, there have been several other women who, through their strong leadership or example, have thoroughly influenced me—women who have opened doors for me and given me encouragement. These dear ones are in my thoughts constantly. In those I hold close to my heart, regardless of profession or personality, there runs the common thread of their devotion to the Lord. I consider these women to be models of godliness and graciousness.

Such women as Ruth Bell Graham, Joyce Meyer, Kay Arthur, Marilyn Hickey, and Florence Littauer are mentors to women of faith who search for identity in the body of Christ. These mentors have experienced the deeper truths of Jehovah God and are able to impart knowledge to this generation.

Many of these women were used by God to usher me into spiritual awakening. I was continually directed, through word and example, to seek Him with all my heart. I was led to discover that God places such people in our lives to bring His message of love and encouragement. If we stay open to new experiences and people, and truly listen with our hearts, we will be prepared to hear. Mentors are lifelines connecting us with our destiny.

Two women in particular, breathed in by God, impacted my life and brought about a turning point. One of these, Eliza, was at least thirty years my senior, but a woman of such spiritual stature and with whom I connected so strongly that I knew immediately the Lord had sent her to me.

As a Bible teacher for younger women, she was loved and revered by all who knew her. One day in particular, we were meeting in the home of the coach of the University of Georgia. I recall that the room was so crowded I had to sit on the floor, but I was so grateful to be there, literally sitting at the feet of this woman of distinction. I remember thinking how beautiful she looked with her steel-gray hair, piercing blue eyes, and flawless complexion, and how impeccably groomed and dressed she was—the picture of mature beauty.

As she taught, imparting riches from the Bible, I hung on every word, savoring this moment of enlightenment, wishing it could last forever. "There is more to the Christian life than just being born again," she said. "We are to love the Lord above all else, to desire to serve Him and honor Him. If you want the more, I can tell you how to achieve it."

As I listened to Eliza, it seemed the Lord, too, was speaking very clearly—from His Word and between the lines: *Love this woman and learn from her, for I have something for you to do that will bless many people. You will be moving into your own calling.*

I was stunned by this revelation but listened on, hoping I would hear something else that would clarify what this meant. The full meaning didn't come forth that day. But

Eliza gave me wonderful advice when I married John. She suggested that I allow my husband to serve me. I knew the deeper meaning of her wisdom. Southern women of my era love to serve others. It is part of our culture to apply the social graces in any situation, and it is the godly thing to do. Eliza was advising me not only to be a giver, but a gracious receiver. I took her advice. Both John and I have benefited.

Another mentor was Mary Crum, who opened up to me a deeper understanding of my spiritual gifts and where I fit into God's plan. Mary and her husband are nationally recognized pastors who have been greatly blessed by this world's standards, and who share liberally with others. They live on a large estate with a barn that has been converted to a church and training center. All are welcome to come here to attend Bible studies and prayer meetings.

It was Mary who first pointed out that my love of transformation could operate in the spiritual realm as well as the material. "That's why you get so excited when people begin to change," she explained to me. She also identified other spiritual gifts and the courage to face all obstacles. These insightful words encouraged me to launch out into the deep with the Lord and to use my design firm as a platform for the transformation of lives, as He would lead.

At this stage of my life, I can look back and reflect on those who were there to help me along the way. Parents, grandparents, teachers, piano tutors, family friends and, as I grew older, business associates, employees, my husband, and of course, Eliza and Mary.

I know that I have had just the right people in my life at every turn of the road. These people have affirmed me, but most of all they have been there to give me direction. These positive role models are so important—people who embrace life and eagerly stretch to reach all that God has planned for them and for those whose lives they touch.

The Mature Years

Heirloom: *"White hair is a crown of glory and is seen most among the godly."*
—Proverbs 16:31

Scripture tells us that wisdom comes with age and life experiences. It also instructs older women to share the lessons of their lives with younger women, to teach them that aging isn't so bad and definitely not something to be feared. To teach them to love their husbands and be "keepers of the home." To teach them that the best is yet to come and that there is a reason for every season—each one a treasure.

In Ecclesiastes (3:1-3 NIV), we find that there is a time for everything, arranged and ordained by God:

> There is a time for everything,
> and a season for every activity under heaven:
> a time to be born and a time to die,
> a time to plant and a time to uproot,
> a time to kill and a time to heal,
> a time to tear down and a time to build.

Sharing with others the lessons we have learned is key to our continuing growth. We often learn our greatest lessons through teaching. This is one reason for writing this book. As I share my personal journey, I want to learn how it takes shape in the lives of my friends, family, and those I have yet to meet.

My gift to you is everything I have come to be through Jesus Christ my Lord. Not merely my gift for interior design, but the Master Designer's touch for your life as well.

❧

There is nothing like experience to teach a lesson. I don't know about you, but once is enough to do it wrong. I have often heard complaints from women who have chosen the wrong colors or fabrics for some room in their house. After a short time they grew tired of those colors or fabrics for some reason. Either because they were too dull, too bright, or "just not me."

Experience is vital when you are working on a commercial design project. This was the case when I met Judy Henry, who is associated with Kay Arthur's Precept Ministries. Judy and I worked together to select the paint colors, lay out the commercial lighting, and choose the furnishings that would be placed in the large lobby in the conference center. My previous experience in commercial projects gave her a great deal of peace. Knowing the end result of using a particular wall color in a huge space is valuable and time-saving, since the wrong color in such proportions could be disastrous. Thus it was wise to call in an expert to help with the decision-making.

Wisdom is the understanding of what is true, right, or lasting. Basically it is simple good judgment and common sense. We are told in the Scriptures to seek wisdom with all our hearts. When God asked Solomon to ask for the one thing he desired above all else, the answer was, "Wisdom." His prayer, of course, was answered; King Solomon's wisdom is legendary.

God is all-wise. He knows everything. From beginning to end, He has purposed the plan for our lives. The wisdom of this world is foolishness compared to the wisdom of God.

In His wisdom, He tells us something about our homes. He says that a house divided against itself will not stand (see Luke 11:17) and that a house without a secure foundation will fall. He also informs us that "the wise woman builds her house, but the foolish pulls it down with her hands"

(Proverbs 14:1 NKJV). A woman's "hands" implies her actions or behavior. What she says and does, what she feels and conveys to others around her can build up or tear down. In other words, one woman—the heart of her home—can either be a construction company or a demolition squad!

Older, wiser women know how costly mistakes can be. We have lived a long time. We have won and lost. We have laughed and cried. We have much to share. Hear us.

Spiritual Daughters

> Heirloom: *"O God, you have helped me from my earliest childhood....Now that I am old and gray, don't forsake me. Give me time to tell this new generation (and their children too) about all your mighty miracles."*
> —Psalm 71:17,18

I remember holding my first child, Courtney, in my arms only hours after she was born. I started speaking to her then and I haven't stopped since. Ours has been such a dear mentoring relationship.

A mother usually has more influence over her daughters than any other woman. In everything she does, she is preparing her children for adulthood, setting the standards for their future home.

Once when I came home from boarding school as a teenager, I found that my room had been beautifully redecorated. Mother had chosen peach floral wallpaper with ferns and flowers everywhere. It was very pretty—although I didn't particularly like the colors and wouldn't have chosen them for myself. There was nothing at all unacceptable about the room—it just wasn't me. My mother's goal had been to complete her redecorating project when it would least inconvenience my sister and me. It probably never occurred to her to include me in the selection process.

When my own daughters came along, I remembered this and decided to involve them in the decorating decisions for their rooms, even though they were under five at the time. "I like this, Mommy" was music to my ears as we chose fabric and wallpaper.

Think about the things you want to pass on to your daughters. Are they learning the deeper lessons of life as well as good interior design and lovely manners? Do they know how their grandparents met, your mother's funniest moment, and other family stories?

Will they know how to set up their own households when the time comes? I don't know what I would have done without my mother's expertise. She moved all four of her children into our respective houses, arriving at our doorstep on moving day, equipped with helpers and painters and whatever else was needed. Mother was the commander of a small army on a mission of mercy. It's one of my favorite memories.

But my mother did far more for us than teach us about homemaking. She followed the biblical exhortation to train up her children in the admonition of the Lord. She taught us the commandments and wisdom of God. She modeled hospitality and instructed us to be good citizens, to put on compassion, kindness, humility, gentleness, and patience. We learned how to forgive and to live together in unity.

Sadly, many women have not had the guidance they have needed. Either their mothers couldn't or wouldn't teach, love, and instruct their daughters; so many women are emotionally unavailable to their children.

Some have lost their mothers to death. A close friend, whose mother died when she was a teenager, sweetly invited me to point out anything that her mother would have taught during those last teenage years, especially in matters of etiquette. Of course I agreed but, to this day, I haven't felt the need to tell her anything. Her request did, however, cause me to ponder the value of a mother's instruction and how much she is missed when she's gone.

These are among the reasons so many women mentors are presently being used mightily by God. When I mentioned Kay Arthur's name to a lady, she quickly responded, "She's my spiritual mother." Kay had never met this dear woman, but through Kay's video lectures and books she has "mothered" others in their Christian faith. She has many, many spiritual children.

One of the most precious aspects of mentoring is the feeling that those under your care become like your children—beloved, encouraged, restored, and sent forth into the world with their vision a little clearer and in focus.

In celebrating life, we truly pass on to the next generation wisdom that could be of great benefit. Maybe we will teach such great lessons and younger women will learn so well that they can avoid the pitfalls we suffered at their age. Many will cherish the opportunity to connect with the older generation. Think what we could all learn from each other. Older women could be inspired by the energy and optimism of the young; younger women could profit from our wisdom and learn from our mistakes. It's funny how this works, isn't it? By giving freely, from your heart, of what you have learned, you ensure that the knowledge and truth you have gained are passed on.

Passing the Torch

Heirloom: *"The younger generation*
will come knocking at my door."

—Henrik Ibsen

God has a special purpose and a plan for the later years. This should be the most fulfilling time of our lives, ripe with challenge and adventure and exciting opportunities to help others. When we know our purpose, we can then effectively mentor those who have been brought under us for a season.

In mid-life, I have found myself desiring to share with younger women. I will gladly offer the benefit of my experience if it will spare them some error in judgment or painful decision, or help them be successful in the home and life they are building.

If you, too, have reached this stage of life, you will not have to search for someone to mentor. At the right time and the right place, God will send her. You will recognize her when she comes to you; you will be recognized when you bring to her your wisdom tempered with love. You will give and receive, share the lessons you have learned and in doing so, learn of the obstacles others have struggled to overcome. It's a kind of two-person study group. You learn from each other. You help each other.

We often hear that kindness begets kindness and love begets love. Believe it! When you give freely of yourself and act only lovingly and joyously toward others, you are teaching them, by example, to do the same. The old saying, "What goes around, comes around," is very true. You can never know how your words or actions may affect someone or some circumstance. You may just be that ray of hope someone has prayed for. Think of the times in your own life when someone, friend or stranger, touched your heart or brought an answer to prayer.

A good mentor will naturally look for the special abilities within those in their charge. Others can often see things about us that we cannot. A friend told me that my words of encouragement had helped her gain the confidence to speak in front of large groups. I didn't even remember the conversation, but she certainly did!

When we encourage others, we impart hope to them. Without hope, there is only fear and despair. But with it, one's creativity level soars to its highest point. It is also true that when we inspire others, we ourselves are freshly inspired.

Several years ago my two daughters, Courtney and Margo, hosted a birthday luncheon for me and invited about seventy lady friends. As the luncheon got under way, each person shared something personal about me. I was so touched to hear them mention incidents in which I had influenced each of them. One precious friend revealed that I had encouraged her to paint more and to exhibit her work in an art gallery. When she did so, a whole new career opened to her. Having recognized her gifts and talents, I knew she needed to move to the next level. What may seem an insignificant gifting to you can be life-changing to someone else.

Teach younger women to ask, "What do you see in me? What do you think are my strong spiritual traits? How can I use them for good and for the cause of Christ?" Cause them to look *within* to identify their giftings, and then to look *up* for the answers to how to use those giftings.

You never know when God will use you as a role model for others. A simple kindness, a word of encouragement, a godly example—or a season of strong teaching and guidance—can enormously impact a life. Look for these opportunities. They are all around you. Then at the proper time, encourage those sitting under you to move into mentoring others. It is time to pass the torch!

13

Reflections

Heirloom: *"A life without
reflection is not worth living."*

—Mark Twain

My mother, now in her late seventies, is at her all-time
loveliest. A petite woman, she carries herself with the regal
assurance of royalty. And well she should. After all, like each
of our sisters in Christ, she is a daughter of the King!

Radiating from these Spirit-led women is a mature beauty
that defies age or circumstance. That aura is the life of Christ
who dwells in them. He makes all things new.

In the peak years we have much to ponder. To rush
through life without moments of contemplation is to deny
the marvel of our Deity. It is to sell our birthright as a child
of royalty in exchange for a bowl of porridge. To be driven by
the urgent rather than guided by self-control is to live by
what the Bible calls "the flesh." It is wise to reflect on all that
has gone before and all that is to be.

The Secret Self

Looking at your reflection in a mirror reveals only the most superficial part of who you really are. The body is the shell of the true self—the covering for the spirit that will live forever. Only God knows the full extent of what you have become and what He has destined you to be.

Within your soul may be sinful desires, selfish ambitions, and secret sins that still must be confessed and forgiven. Now is the time. Don't wait another day, another moment to repent of anything that keeps you from full commitment to the Lord. He is ready to cleanse and forgive in order to prepare you for the next phase of life, the next promotion.

Also deep within may be precious treasure yet to be mined. The giftings God has given you are to be used, not closeted away. Discover all you can be, then determine to begin. It is never too late to learn more about yourself. Never too late to receive more of Him. Keep studying His Word. Keep praying. Keep praising and thanking Him. He wants to use you in ever increasing ways to champion His kingdom and bring glory to His name. He has more for you. Receive it!

A dear old saint, who had served the Lord faithfully for many years, was overheard on his deathbed, confessing, "I am so grateful that the Lord can still teach an old man." He continued to grow spiritually and to remain vibrant and alive, despite pain and weakness, until the last day of his life.

Dreams may be buried deep inside your heart, dreams that seem impossible because you are no longer young enough for the energy to make them come true. It might have worked had you started earlier or worked harder or been more tuned in to God's plan for your life. But you're no spring chicken. It's almost winter.

T. D. Jakes writes about "winter women" in his best-selling book, *Woman, Thou Art Loosed:*

> God never extends life beyond purpose....Sarah
> didn't take 'faith' classes. She just went through
> her winter clutching the warm hand of a loving
> God who could not fail. So when you hear Sarah
> laughing...she is laughing with God. She is
> holding her baby to her wrinkled breast. And
> she understands the miracles that come only to
> winter women.

Stand in openness and transparency before the God who created you and numbered your days. He counts time differently from mortals. This season may be a beginning, not an ending. He is only waiting for you to acknowledge that you need Him as never before. He is not through with you.

As I was struggling with the imminent death of my sister, my sleep patterns were sporadic. Often I would awaken after only two or three hours of sleep to the sober reality of her death. Instead of disturbing John, I would ease out of bed and wander through the house, praying softly or rearranging accessories in a room. Therapy.

John, who is also a very light sleeper, would soon come and find me, give me a kiss, and comfort me with the reminder that God is in control and His ways are higher than ours, that if we put our trust in God, we can be at peace.

Even with this comfort my sleep was still erratic, until amazingly I slept through the night peacefully, awaking to feel deeply refreshed.

It was then John told me that during the night, I had tossed and turned so restlessly that he had walked around to my side of the bed, stood over me, and prayed quietly until I fell into a deep sleep.

I was so touched by this precious gesture. "How long did you stand there praying, Honey?" I asked.

"Oh, for quite awhile. It's not the first time, you know," he replied with a smile. "I often pray for you like that."

I felt quick tears spring to my eyes. How like the Lord John's silent vigil seemed. The One who knows us best and loves us most hovers over us, covering and protecting us while we sleep, quieting us with His love (see Zephaniah 3:17).

The Seventh Day

Heirloom: *"On the seventh day,*
having finished his task, God ceased from
this work he had been doing, and God
blessed the seventh day and declared
it holy, because it was the day
when he ceased this work of creation."

—Genesis 2:2

Productivity is part of God's plan, of course. Quietude and reflection are equally dimensions of that grand design, beginning with the Creation story; God built the first home and created its occupants in six days, then rested on the seventh. Reflecting on the activity of the six days, He pronounced it "good." God was satisfied with His work, but after He had finished, He took one day to consider what He had done. In resting after His creative enterprise, He was establishing the pattern for human life.

Slowing down the mind and body is a boundary of living given for our protection in the Ten Commandments.

To violate this commandment wreaks havoc with the human soul and body.

A woman is finely wired to operate in this physical world. If she neglects the needs of her body, emotional and mental fatigue can set in and cause depression. By the time a woman is ministering, she has often experienced brokenness. At those times, she was totally dependent on the Lord to give her rest and renewal. Now she probably knows her limits and plans pockets of peace each day—time to be alone with the Lord and receive rest.

The rhythms of life are seen in nature and the animal kingdom. Horses and mules cannot work all day without rest. Bears hibernate in winter, trees shed their leaves, and plant life is dormant during the winter. The human body needs eight hours of sleep. Working overtime robs a person of family time and reflection. Without the proper rest and recreation, a woman cannot function at her optimum level.

There is also that time after trauma when the pace of life is interrupted to allow for a breather. A death, divorce, breakdown—any time of grief—shuts the body down for a season. Moses spent forty years in the desert as a shepherd, after running for his life from the scene of a murder he committed in Egypt.

During those years of tending sheep, Moses had time to reflect on his upbringing and his purpose in life. As an Israelite, reared in the palace of an Egyptian Pharaoh, he learned that his destiny involved freeing his people from the oppression of Egypt. His rash actions, untempered by wisdom, however, caused him to flee to the mountains. Moses' zeal was replaced with God's passion. Human zeal may result in burnout; God's passion will endure forever.

In Green Pastures

Heirloom: *"The Lord is my Shepherd...*
He makes me to lie down in green pastures.
He leads me beside the still waters."

—Psalm 23:1,2 (NKJV)

Keeping late hours, eating improperly, not exercising regularly, and neglecting other health issues will promote poor health. Like so many others, you may not have learned these basic lessons earlier in your life and may now feel powerless to halt these bad patterns and addictive behaviors. Sometimes the Good Shepherd rescues His sheep when they are running headlong down a destructive path by permitting an illness or some other setback. Setbacks are divine set-ups. During the time of recovery, you will be forced to pause long enough to rest and reflect on those things that are of true value.

Even good works can crowd out God's best. Satan's strategy is to pervert and divert. Is it possible that you are participating in too many prayer groups or seminars, or helping others when your own household needs your attention? Be sure that you are hearing the voice of the Lord and that you follow His leading, and His alone.

The Greek word for *rest* means "useful." It is useful to be yoked with Jesus. His ways are restful, light, and easy. He does not place on your shoulders that which He isn't willing to help you carry. He is not seeking worldly or religious approval. He wants only to please His Father in heaven, and His Father is not a harsh taskmaster.

Our flesh and the devil want to drive us to death. Fortunately, death to the flesh is God's plan, also, so that His children can be released to work with His strength and not their own. In times of weariness, find the most peaceful spot in your house—your private sanctuary—and meditate on these words: "They that wait upon the Lord shall renew their strength. They shall mount up with wings like eagles; they shall run and not be weary; they shall walk and not faint" (Isaiah 40:31).

Waiting Before the Lord

Deborah was an Old Testament woman who knew the value of reflection. At a time in history when the children of Israel had no king and "everyone did what was right in his own eyes," God used a woman to lead them home to Him.

When their enemies threatened to overcome the Israelites, they would repent and cry out to God for deliverance, and He would send a judge or great leader to help them. Deborah was a wife and mother as well as a prophetess and judge, raised up by the Lord for such a time.

Sitting in her outdoor parlor, shaded by a palm tree, she sought the Lord and received great wisdom and insight for His wayward people. Following God's orders, she advised the military leader Barak as to battle strategy, then accompanied him to the battlefield to help carry it out.

Deborah was a woman who waited before the Lord in reflection and prayer, seeking His counsel in a day of cultural confusion. She was available to be used when there were no men stepping up to the plate. She called herself "a mother in Israel" whose heart was with Israel's rulers (see Judges 5:7, 9). This is similar to the godly women of today, who pray for our leaders, but who are willing to be "politically incorrect" and speak out against cultural sins.

Today's women of prayer can alter the course of current events. Shirley Dobson coordinates the National Day of Prayer, a time when millions of Americans pray for national repentance and revival. Like the sun rising, so is the effective, fervent prayer of a righteous woman which avails much. Hearts are strengthened, marriages restored, bodies healed, and relationships mended.

Martha and Mary, two New Testament sisters, are examples of the value the Lord places on reflection. When Jesus dropped by their house for a visit with His friends, Martha busied herself in the kitchen, complaining when her sister lingered with their Guest instead of coming to help. The honored Guest Himself noticed Martha's "busyness" and scolded her gently, saying, "Martha, Martha, you are worried and troubled about many things. But one thing is needed, and Mary has chosen that good part, which will not be taken away from her" (Luke 10:41,42 NKJV).

The condition of the house was not the issue with Jesus; it was the condition of the heart—being busy about the Father's business—that mattered to Him. True fulfillment comes when a woman occupies herself with "that good part, which will not be taken away from her."

Filled and Fulfilled

Heirloom: *"The whole purpose of Jesus' ministry is to bring us to the house of His Father...Jesus wants us to be where he is."*

—Henri Nouwen

In the Japanese culture, life is divided into three parts. The first stage includes birth, childhood, and education. As with the Japanese, so it is with us. During this stage, we are taught and mentored. From parents and grandparents, we are exposed to life in its entirety. We learn from their experience and their example. This is the beginning of being filled.

For most people, as with the Japanese, marriage and family mark the second stage. We begin a life with someone else, leaving our birth family and uniting with another. We build a family unit and a home. We work hard to arrange our house and accomplish our goals. This is a continuation of being filled and filling others.

In both Japanese and American cultures, the mature years comprise the third and final stage of life. Here we reap the rewards of all our hard work—both materially and spiritually. As we have planted the seeds of loving and living, we will reap a harvest of that planting. This is the time of replenishment and fulfillment. We are filled full.

Something very odd happened when I realized I was entering the final stage of life. Something completely unexpected. At a luncheon for businesswomen, where I had been asked to introduce the keynote speaker of the day, I heard this startling statistic, "If you have lived to be fifty in good health, you can expect to reach the age of ninety-seven."

Immediately, I began doing some mental calculation. If that statistic were true, then I was only *halfway* through my life! These years have already been extremely satisfying, but I am beginning to feel that there is much, much more to come—the best!

For several years as I spoke and lectured in various settings, I heard repeatedly, "You ought to write a book." Not having felt a particular gifting in this area, I put it out of my mind. So no one was more surprised than I to find myself writing in addition to running my design business. My love for people and for God has led naturally to yet another medium for expressing His transforming power in the lives of those I meet. At this point I am the author of six books, with others in the conceptual stage. It is truly one of the most enjoyable and productive phases of my life.

I am finding, too, that God is equipping me with the gifts needed for this new undertaking. He is releasing fresh anointing and sending people to stand with me in prayer and to assist me with their giftings.

For others who may have been "pushed out of the nest" by premature retirement through loss of a job, don't panic. Consider what God may be doing for you. You may have actually received a promotion—from the Lord!

🌺

A friend of mine who commanded a high-level executive job in the city was suddenly let go. Just over fifty, she was still as capable as ever and much more experienced than the newcomers on the business scene. In the face of this setback, my friend's faith faltered momentarily. She felt used up, passed over, and completely inadequate. A failure.

I reminded her that she was forgetting to trust God, who knows all things and has a purpose for every life. That she needed to take another look at the possibilities inherent in this situation.

"OK," she said, drawing in a deep breath. "I didn't mean to whine. I'll look for the silver lining and move on."

Within months my friend had established her own consulting firm, drawing on her many years of experience in the business. Clients began to gravitate to her. And now my friend is finding that God is blessing her three-fold in both income and satisfaction.

Each stage in our spiritual walk leads down the pathway of destiny. Sometimes the journey is long and the road dark and treacherous. At other times we feel the hope and anticipation of knowing we are almost there. God's plan includes a roadmap—the Bible—for the narrow road that leads to a purposed destination. Don't be detoured by circumstances. Trust Him to lead you all the way Home.

Through a Glass Darkly

Heirloom: *"We can see and understand
only a little about God now, as if we were
peering at his reflection in a poor mirror;
but someday we are going to see him in his
completeness, face to face."*

—1 Corinthians 13:12

There are so many things I still don't understand. Why
Ann Lee had to die of cancer at the age of nineteen. Why my
sister had to be taken from her husband and baby while she
was a young woman. So many mind-boggling questions. So
few answers.

The ancient mirrors mentioned in the thirteenth chapter
of First Corinthians were actually made of metal, manufac-
tured in Corinth, which gave only a dim reflection. The
verse goes on to say, "Now all that I know is hazy and
blurred, but then I will see everything clearly, just as clearly
as God sees into my heart right now" (verse 12b). Someday,
when we behold Him face to face, we will understand many
things—about life, about God, and about our future with
Him and those who have gone before.

In the meantime, we view everything through our dis-
torted perception. Incomplete understanding drives us to
our knees, to Abba Father, who will comfort and counsel as
only He can. We will never have all the answers this side of
heaven. But we can trust the Father who does—and help
bring healing to others.

❧

The mother of a friend collected teacups and saucers for
each of her daughter's birthdays. My friend was only sixteen
when her mother died, and the estate was settled while she

was away in boarding school. The teacup collection was given to a sister-in-law by mistake, and never returned.

Years later, still heartbroken over the loss of her mother, my friend told me this story. I determined to think of a way to help her heal.

By the time her birthday rolled around ten months later, I had come up with an idea. I hosted a birthday luncheon and invited twelve of her closest friends to bring a cup and saucer to recreate the collection she had lost, asking each of them to make their selection based on some personal characteristic of the giver. I wanted my friend to "see" those who loved her as she viewed her new collection.

As my friend unwrapped each dear teacup, we, her closest friends, became vessels of healing for her. The look in her eyes spoke volumes about the emotions she was feeling. The party was a great success, with tears and laughter flowing like a river.

As restoration and healing begin, we feel the presence of the Lord. He cares about all the missing teacups in our lives. He wants us to know Him as Redeemer and Restorer of precious things. Keep looking to Him, the Author and Finisher of our faith!

14

Spiritual Heirlooms

✓ Heirloom: *"God's secret plan, now at last made known, is Christ himself. In him lie hidden all the mighty, untapped treasures of wisdom and knowledge."*

—Colossians 2:2,3

*H*eritage, estate, inheritance, treasure, lineage. These words paint a picture of generational bonds of love. We inherit much more from our ancestors than material possessions. More than our mother's eyes and our father's smile. We receive a spiritual inheritance as well.

Like the beloved family possessions that are carefully handed down from one generation to the next, our parents and grandparents bequeath a priceless legacy of moral, social, and spiritual values that make a society and a home function properly.

When I was a child, a visit to Charleston to see Grandmother Winnie usually included a visit to the museum. There we would wander the halls, viewing the treasures on display and reading all about the history of the fabulous pieces.

From this grandmother and from my mother, whose collections included silver, glass, and other rare objets d'art, I inherited a love of beautiful things.

But my appreciation for beauty extends far beyond art, architecture, and fine antiques. I value most the beloved faces of my family, sweet relationships with friends, and above all, the deep things of the Spirit. These are my true treasures, cherished heirlooms of the heart.

The spiritual truths I have gained—not the paintings and porcelains—will constitute my richest legacy to my heirs. I want them to remember me on my knees, as a woman of prayer. I have never dictated my children's or my grandchildren's lives, but have left them in the loving arms of their heavenly Father and trusted Him to fulfill their destiny.

Just to check my progress in this respect, I once asked my nine-year-old grandson, Dickson, to describe me in his own words. Of course it was a bold request on my part—not knowing what he might say. I had already learned from my granddaughter, Ivey, who had written the report on Grandparents' Day, that she thought I was a "good listener." Now I wanted to know what Dickson thought.

He pressed his finger to his cheek and rolled his eyes heavenward in studied concentration. "Well, Grammy, I think you're gentle...." He thought some more. "And you're an optimist...and you smell good!"

I wasn't too sure Dickson understood the definition of the word *optimist*, but when I quizzed him, he recited the meaning straight out of Webster's Dictionary, and I learned that this had been his "word for the day" at school. *A gentle optimist—who smells good.*

Well I suppose that is a worthy tribute, especially if my grandson was referring to the fragrance of the Lord. For that is my desired aim—to leave behind the pleasing aroma of a prayerful life, centered on Christ and devoted to others.

❧

Our lives, like our homes, with all their material and spiritual belongings, are given to us to occupy or use for a season. The passing on of these possessions is the inheritance handed down to the next generation. Whether what we pass on is positive or negative is our choice. We will not be taking material things with us. There is no U-Haul to heaven!

Birthright

Heirloom: *"Yes, dear friends, we are already God's children, right now, and we can't even imagine what it is going to be like later on."*

—1 John 3:2

Before we can pass on treasures, we must first receive them. Sometimes this comes by way of an inheritance bequeathed to you from someone in your family line. What are you expecting to inherit? The family estate—that can burn or be destroyed in a hurricane or a tornado? A diamond ring or an emerald necklace—that can be stolen or lose its luster? A portfolio of stocks and bonds—that can depreciate overnight?

Material assets are important. To sustain life and enjoy a measure of comfort, we need some of the things money can buy. But all that this world has to offer is equivalent to nothing more than a pauper's legacy, while God has promised you a fortune! As children of the King, we are joint heirs with Christ and, as such, shall inherit all the riches of heaven.

When my mother became ill a number of years ago and awaited a heart bypass, my sister-in-law and I reviewed Mother's will. I was shocked to learn at that time that none of her jewelry, including a stunning double strand of pearls that my father had given her, was being left to me, but to my niece, instead.

Never having felt unloved or deprived of anything that was within my mother's power to give me, I could not understand. Oh, not that it really mattered. I had all the jewelry I needed, including some lovely pieces John had given me for birthdays and other special occasions. But I was hurt by this, and I had to pray it through, asking God to reveal to me why she had chosen to bypass her natural daughter.

In the meantime, with Mother's surgery looming ahead, I put this thought out of my mind and set about to think of ways to make her recovery as pleasant as possible. She withstood the surgery surprisingly well and was soon out of danger, surrounded by family, friends, and a staff of nurses and household helpers to care for her.

A few months later, John and I began making plans for Christmas, which was right around the corner. We decided to spend the holidays at the mountain house, where we could combine some rest time with a meaningful observation of the sacred season.

For some reason, John kept wanting to pin me down about the exact time we would be arriving. In my preoccupation with Mother's condition and with wrapping up some design business before the holidays, I gave him a date, then promptly forgot all about it.

On the twenty-second of December, after we arrived in the mountains on schedule, a FedEx delivery was made—an early Christmas gift from John. Inside the package was a double strand of pearls so magnificent they literally took my breath away! So much finer and more lustrous than any I had ever seen. It was as if my husband had made a trip to the South Seas and hand-selected each pearl, then wrapped the gift in love and tenderness.

I was once again reminded of the goodness of God. He has so much more for us than our natural inheritance. Instead of inheriting pearls from my mother, I received them directly from my Father—through the husband of my heart.

When the will is read, and you are left out, look for the higher truth. Your Father in heaven has more for you—much more. All "His riches in glory by Christ Jesus" (Philippians 4:19 NKJV)...and the finer pearls!

Eternal Inheritance

The spiritual inheritance bequeathed by our Father to His children, those who believe in Him and trust Him, is nothing less than eternal life with Christ in heaven. This realm is beyond imagination, but we know by faith that it is true and real.

As believers, we have made deposits in heaven—in faith, hope, love, mercy, and forgiveness toward others—that we may be unaware of. Each time we give a gift of time or treasure without expecting a return, each time we make an investment in someone's life or ministry, each time we speak a word of encouragement we are making a deposit in heaven. The Word tells us that our words and deeds are recorded, and that our tears and prayers are stored in golden bowls. But these deeds and prayers do not earn us a ticket to heaven. "Salvation is not a reward for the good we have done, so none of us can take any credit for it. It is God himself who has made us what we are and given us new lives from Christ Jesus" (Ephesians 2:9,10).

Spend some time in reliving your conversion experience. Think about the time and place, the person or persons who led you to Jesus. How did you feel? What did you say and do immediately afterward? It is that freshness we want to recover in our maturing years, for God's most precious gift is ever new.

> All honor to God, the God and Father of our Lord Jesus Christ; for it is his boundless mercy that has given us the privilege of being born again, so that we are now members of God's own family. Now we live in the hope of eternal life because Christ rose again from the dead. And God has reserved for his children the priceless gift of eternal life; it is kept in heaven for you, pure and undefiled, beyond the reach of change and decay.
>
> —1 Peter 1:3,4

Salvation from sin and the hope of heaven—this is our true inheritance, one that will last for all eternity. Our mortal minds cannot conceive of the length of eternity—a time with no beginning and no end. A person, now anonymous, once attempted to describe it this way: "If a tiny bird flew to the top of a mountain made of diamonds, the hardest substance known to man, and brushed it lightly with a feather each hundred years, by the time that mountain was reduced to dust, it would be only the morning of eternity."

Our spiritual heritage is guaranteed. Just as kings and queens once sealed important documents and letters with a signet ring, so our destiny is sealed by the Holy Spirit.

> Because of what Christ did, all you others too, who heard the Good News about how to be saved, and trusted Christ, were marked as belonging to Christ by the Holy Spirit, who long ago had been promised to all of us Christians. His presence

within us is God's guarantee that he really will
give us all that he promised; and the Spirit's seal
upon us means that God has already purchased
us and that he guarantees to bring us to himself.
This is just one more reason for us to praise our
glorious God.

—Ephesians 1:13,14

Divine Integrity

Heirloom: *"A genuine faith is
always a practical faith."*

—Elisabeth Elliot

I have made a will, of course. In this day and time, it
simply saves confusion to list one's assets and state how they
are to be distributed after one's death. There will be some
treasures and real estate that I have enjoyed and will hand
down to my daughters and my grandchildren.

But it is who I am and what I believe that is most important. Above all else, I desire to be a woman of integrity.
Integrity is all about character, dependability, honesty, and
truth. It is who we are when no one else is around. It is a
standard of values set by the code of God's Word.

Integrity, along with faith, prayer, and love, are among
the heirlooms I want to pass down to my heirs. You probably
know of someone who lacks integrity, thinking they can get
away without being accountable for their actions. These
people lack the ability to follow God's standard of excellence.

Once, when having difficulty with a client concerning a
business matter, I consulted with my father. This client had
been dishonest with me, and I was at a loss as to how to

handle it. He listened patiently while I tried to explain the problem, and as I finished, I asked, "What would you do?"

Daddy leaned back in his chair, peered over his glasses at me, and replied firmly, "I wouldn't do business with her."

It had never occurred to me that I had a choice in the matter. I quickly ended the association with this client and was greatly relieved.

Our heavenly Father also gives us options. We can choose to associate with unprincipled people and hang out in questionable places, or we can keep ourselves pure and unspotted from the world. I want my descendants to remember me as a woman of principle who held to high standards of conduct, both in business and at home.

Elisabeth Elliot tells of a headmistress in the boarding school she attended who said, " 'Don't go around with a Bible under your arm if you don't sweep under your bed.' She was looking for a genuine faith. She wanted no spiritual talk coming out of a messy room."

I want my descendants to know that "I practice what I preach." That I have cleaned up the "messy rooms" of my life and that my faith is an authentic faith. I want them to know that I have always refused to compromise and that people can set their watches by my word. In this world of ethical and moral instability, I want to be a firm anchor for their souls and to point them to the Rock of Ages who will never let them down.

Royal Treasures

While visiting London, John and I had the opportunity to see the crown jewels of the Windsor Dynasty, housed in the Tower of London since the beginning of the fourteenth century. This display of jewels and royal regalia, including the coronation crowns of English kings and queens through the ages, is one of the most impressive in the world.

As I have studied the Bible, that richest repository of treasures for the believer, I have learned some interesting facts about crowns. Crowns are worn to mark a person's high status and authority. Jesus is portrayed in the Book of Revelation as wearing many crowns, signifying His kingly authority (see 19:12). We, as inhabitants of the kingdom of God, "shall also be a crown of glory in the hand of the Lord, and a royal diadem in the hand of your God" (Isaiah 62:3 NKJV).

The Apostle Paul writes of the Christian:

> Do you not know that those who run in a race all run, but one receives the prize? Run in such a way that you may obtain it. And everyone who competes for the prize is temperate in all things. Now they do it to obtain a perishable crown, but we for an imperishable crown.
>
> —1 Corinthians 9: 24,25 (NKJV)

If we persevere in the race of life, we win a crown—and not just any crown, an "imperishable crown," one that will endure. The Living Bible explains it this way: "An athlete goes to all this trouble just to win a blue ribbon or a silver cup, but we do it for a heavenly reward that never disappears." The condition for receiving the crown is self-denial and temperance.

James has more to say about our heavenly inheritance: "Happy is the [woman] who doesn't give in and do wrong when [she] is tempted, for afterwards [she] will get as [her] reward the crown of life that God has promised those who love him" (1:12). Enduring temptation is another prerequisite for receiving our heavenly reward, yet James makes it very clear that whatever it takes to acquire this crown will bring sublime happiness. It's worth the effort!

ஜ

The exhibit in the Tower of London also includes rare and exquisite jewels. The Imperial Crown of State features an uncut ruby and four tear-shaped pearls, along with seventeen sapphires, eleven emeralds, and five other rubies. The uncut ruby, once owned by the King of Granada, has a long and intriguing history, having been lost and rediscovered more than once. The Scepter with the Cross is topped by the largest of the Stars of Africa, the largest diamond ever mined, and nearly three thousand smaller diamonds.

While this display in the Tower of London is breathtaking, the breastplate worn by the high priest Aaron in Old Testament times was equally dramatic. Over a fine linen ephod woven with gold, scarlet, purple, and blue threads was a breastplate studded with twelve precious stones arranged in four rows, representing the twelve tribes of Israel: ruby, topaz, emerald, tourquoise, sapphire, diamond, amber, agate, amethyst, onyx, beryl, jasper—all set in gold.

Each stone was prized for its beauty, rarity, and durability. The diamond, composed of pure crystallized carbon, formed under conditions of extreme heat and pressure deep within the earth, is the hardest mineral known and, of all earthly materials, will endure longest.

The emerald found in Egypt, Cyprus, and Ethiopia was a deep green variety of beryl, and was used as an article of trade in ancient times. We will see a rainbow, resembling the brilliance of an emerald, surrounding the throne of God.

The ruby is valued for its beauty and clarity. Even though rubies were exchanged for other items in early times and even today are used for decoration and embellishment, wisdom is more to be desired. "She [wisdom] is more precious than rubies, and all the things you may desire cannot compare with her" (Proverbs 3:15 NKJV). A woman of wisdom knows the temporal nature of this world's wealth and has transferred her account to heaven.

Upon each stone on the front of Aaron's breastplate, like a seal, was engraved the name of one of the tribes of Israel. As the high priest entered the presence of God in the holy place, he carried these names over his heart before the Lord, "as a constant reminder....Thus Jehovah will be reminded of them continually" (Exodus 28:12,29).

Jesus is our Great High Priest. He ever lives to make intercession for us and to be our advocate with the Father. He pleads our case and stands before our Judge, covered in His blood, shed for us. Instead of an ephod and a breastplate, He has written our names in "the palms of His hands" and on His heart. We are never out of His sight or away from His loving presence.

As I recalled our wonderful trip to London, seeing the crown jewels, and as I have studied and mined precious truths from God's Word, I found another breathtaking gem:

> Then those who feared and loved the Lord spoke often of him to each other. And he had a Book of Remembrance drawn up in which he recorded the names of those who feared him and loved to think about him.
>
> 'They shall be mine,' says the Lord of Hosts, 'in that day when I make up my jewels. And I will spare them as a man spares an obedient and dutiful son.'
>
> —Malachi 3:16,17

We are God's jewels! He is gathering us as a display of His love and grace. But we must be willing to undergo the deep refining process that will purge us of impurities and allow His true beauty to shine forth.

My prayer for you is:

> Out of [God's] glorious, unlimited resources he will give you the mighty inner strengthening of his Holy Spirit. And I pray that Christ will be more and more at home in your hearts, living within you as you trust in him. May your roots go down deep into the soil of God's marvelous love; and may you be able to feel and understand, as all God's children should, how long, how wide, how deep, and how high his love really is.
>
> —Ephesians 3:16-19

15

Inivitation to a Wedding

Heirloom: *"The Spirit
and the bride say, 'Come!'
And let him who hears say, 'Come!'"*

—Revelation 22:17 (NKJV)

In the Low Country of South Carolina, *dinner* is at noon. *Supper* is the term reserved for the evening meal—that special time of day when families return to the nest from their day's activities, the time when, for a married couple, troubles are halved and joys are doubled.

It is almost Suppertime, my friend—the Marriage Supper of the Lamb.

Like most women, I do love a beautiful wedding. The delicate fragrance of wedding flowers—roses, lilies, stephanotis, gardenias, lilacs. The romantic music, tender with emotion. The solemn vows exchanged. That mystical moment when the minister pronounces the couple "husband and wife." The anticipation of all that is to come, including the reception after the ceremony—often a wedding supper.

I have been privileged to attend many lovely weddings and receptions, from high-noon formal to country casual. But the Wedding Supper of the Lamb, given by Father God in honor of His Son Jesus and His Bride, the Church, will surpass all others.

The guest list is confined to believers only—those who have embraced Jesus as Savior and Lord, the Lover of our souls. You and I will be there, but this wedding will be unlike any we have ever attended or participated in. We will not be there as guests, but as the Bride, His Church, and we will be dressed to the nines—in a glorious robe of spotless white, without a single wrinkle. This garment is our gift from the Bridegroom, paid for by His own blood, washed in the Word, so that He might present us to Himself, "holy and without blemish" (Ephesians 5:27 NKJV).

What an event! The millennial party to end all parties! When I think of it, I yearn to be there, to see my Lord's sweet face and to feel His arms around me. Yet there is more for me to do here for Him. More to teach my children and grandchildren. More blessings to give and receive. More to learn about the Love of my life....

Deity in Disguise

Heirloom: *"He had a name written that no one knew except Himself....on His robe and on His thigh a name written: KING OF KINGS AND LORD OF LORDS."*
—Revelation 19:12,16 (NKJV)

Who is this King "with eyes like a flame" and crowned with many crowns, who will charge forth on a white steed in the vanguard of the armies of heaven?

He first came to us in disguise. To save them from the brutality of Roman rule, the ancient Israelites were expecting a monarch in the style of David, complete with pomp and pageantry. Instead the King of kings came as a newborn baby, sheltered in a lowly stable. Who would have thought that His Supreme Majesty would appear in such a garb—or be housed so crudely?

Only those of the true family of God would look with spiritual eyes for a spiritual kingdom. Anna, the prophetess, recognized Jesus immediately when His mother and earthly father brought Him to the temple for dedication. Old Simeon, too, declared that he could go to be with God now that he had seen the Messiah. But most of the priests and temple workers were blind to this great blessing, the answer to all their prayers.

❧

Do we have spiritual eyes in our own families? Do we realize that we are living with potential royalty? Does the familiar become commonplace as we pass each other in our homes?

As we moved into our new house this year, I felt an urgent need to get everything unpacked and put away. I wanted to put my home in order so that I could be free to do other things. Early mornings found me unwrapping china, folding guest towels, and placing accessories in our new rooms.

I was rushing to get ready for a celebration—my husband's birthday, which was only three weeks away. Shortly before the day, I called a few friends and invited them to an impromptu dinner party. In advance I gave the guests a tape recorder and asked each one to wish John a happy birthday, adding any remarks they cared to make.

As John listened to his friends speak, telling him how his various spiritual gifts had influenced each of their lives, he was warmed by the affirmation of love and friendship. It was one of the most intimate evenings we have experienced among friends.

John went to sleep that night, blessed by the praise and gratitude of people who love him. I am so thankful that my house was in order at this important time, or we would have missed the blessing.

When we cradle our family members with respect and honor, as Mary cradled the King, we will be growing more like Him, more ready to meet Him when the time is right.

Revelation

Heirloom: *"And I saw a new heaven and a new earth."*
—Revelation 21:1 (NKJV)

Just when we think the picture is complete, God adds some more paint to the canvas. If we were never asked to move out in ministry or to try new things, we would not grow and learn. It is in doing these "new things" that we remain youthful, keep fresh and current—as "dewy-eyed" as a bride—and attain the heights God has for us.

It is never too late to learn. Life, with its seasons and rhythms, is continuously ebbing and flowing, carrying us along toward our final destination. Every turn and bend of the road is a new experience. Wait for the new opportunities that will present themselves. In the right time and season, they will come.

One of the joys of the mature years is the time and desire to dig deeply into God's Word. This is a daily delight, as I refresh my spirit and learn more and more about my divine destination. Exploring the book of Revelation has been an astonishing study. While some feel that this book is too obscure to be understood, too filled with mysterious symbolism, I have found it to be pure joy. The word *revelation* itself is a clue. *Revelation* means "a revealing," not "a cover-up"!

In this great book, the apostle John writes of a heavenly vision that speaks of those things that are yet to come as if he were seeing them with his natural eyes. Yet, because human language is limited, some concepts are too lofty, too dazzling for our finite minds to comprehend. What the apostle saw, inspired by the Holy Spirit, is wrapped in words that are poor vehicles for the vision. But they are enough to strike a chord of response in me!

He saw "the holy city, New Jerusalem, coming down out of heaven from God, prepared as a bride adorned for her husband." The designer in me kicks in when I read the account of this city: "Her light [of the city] was like a most precious stone, like a jasper stone, clear as crystal...and the city was pure gold, like clear glass. The foundations of the wall of the city were adorned with all kinds of precious stones" (Revelation 21:2,11,18,19 NKJV).

As I read of all the jewels adorning the foundation of the walls of the city, I remember that these were the very same stones worn by the high priest to represent the twelve tribes of Israel in the Old Testament. The stones are symbolic of the people dear to God's heart. The jewels represent you and me!

Recalling the fine pearls John had given me for Christmas a few years ago, I always feel teary-eyed when I come to the passage on the gates of the heavenly city. Twelve gates—each one a single, perfect pearl! My mind can scarcely take it in. As a designer, I love gates and entryways, the access point of homes and gardens. To think that I will walk into heaven through a gate of pearl is precious to me.

In heaven there is no need for lighting fixtures or lamps, or even sun or moon, for the city is illuminated by the glory of God, and "the Lamb is its light. And the nations of those who are saved shall walk in its light" (verses 23,24 NKJV).

With this vision ever before us, we can make the most of our remaining years on earth. Keep in mind that your most rewarding years are just ahead, your greatest gifts undiscovered, your most glorious prize waiting to be awarded—and ultimately, your most magnificent house yet to be built.

Coming Home

Heirloom: *"In My Father's house
are many mansions; if it were not so,
I would have told you. I go to prepare
a place for you. And if I go to prepare
a place for you, I will come again
and receive you to Myself."*

—John 14:2,3 (NKJV)

After the wedding, a couple begins to "take up house-keeping," as we say here in the South. Whether a house or apartment, castle or condominium, the newlyweds must begin to make a home for themselves and the children they might desire someday.

In my twenty-five years of interior design, I have had the privilege of decorating many houses. Some of them would qualify as mansions—with many great rooms, including ballrooms, libraries, observatories, and chapels. I have searched the world, including the most prestigious sources in Europe, for the finest fabrics, rugs, artwork, and furnishings. My training and experience have taught me to discern the authentic over the reproduction, the fine over the fake. Many years of searching for beautiful things have rewarded me with a keen eye.

My spiritual eyes have also grown keener as I have matured. What John is telling me through the Book of Revelation is that God has prepared a home for us that is more glorious than anything we could possibly envision. Our heavenly home is filled with beauty, majesty, and splendor beyond earthly imagination. The Lord took our cottage—in need of complete renovation—and gave us His castle. In this castle, we will discover treasures of gold and silver and jewels of great price. There will be no sin, no sorrow—only peace, joy, and love. This is our real and final home.

Regardless of the dysfunction of your past, the hurtful memories and the rejection and abandonment you may have received at the hands of others, you were created with the strong desire to "come Home." God placed that desire in your heart to draw you to His house. There is no person or place on earth that compares.

We shall dwell in this Paradise of eternal joy with the Lord who died for us that we might live. During the building of our eternal homes, He may do some remodeling of hearts and attitudes that will be painful in the process. Keep in mind that He is restoring secret gardens, lost dreams, and forgotten hopes. As the hammer pounds and the chisel shapes, we are being made fit for this celestial kingdom, for nothing that defiles shall enter.

Ever After

Heirloom: *"God himself...will wipe away all tears from their eyes, and there shall be no more death, nor sorrow, nor crying, nor pain. All of that has gone forever."*

—Revelation 21:3,4

The morning my sister died, I joined my parents at "Willbrook." As we made arrangements for the funeral, the care of little Tyler, and other pressing matters, I noticed a peace about Mother that struck me as unusual. A musing sort of look, as if she were entertaining some delightful secret.

When I asked about it, she replied, "Oh, I was just thinking that Mary Ashley must be having a glorious time in heaven right now. I am sure that my mother and Mother Williams have formed a receiving line and are introducing her to her great-great-great grandparents all the way back."

The thought of those two grande dames observing the social graces in the halls of heaven and presenting Mary Ashley to the Charleston society of the centuries brought a smile to my face for the first time in days. What a comfort to know that our family bloodline—as far back as we have traced our roots—is all solidly Christian, believers of the first magnitude. These many generations of family saints were surely gathering around my sister to welcome her to the inner courts of praise.

The husband of Mary Ashley's best friend, Nancy, wrote to my parents soon after my sister's funeral: "If anyone suspects heaven to be dull, it cannot be since Mary Ashley is now there. That same spark and spontaneity that she possessed in this life is now existent in her life in God's presence, and today He must be receiving the joy and delight we had when she lived among us."

What a lovely thing to say. But there was more. "I arrived long before her funeral service began," he went on, "and in prayerful meditation, sat there reflecting on the meaning of the brief experiences I had with Mary Ashley. During those reflective moments it came to me that her true credibility derived from the fact that she never viewed anyone as insignificant. It was then that these words from our Lord kept resounding through my mind: 'I tell you the truth, what you did for one of the least of these brothers of mine, you did for me.' When Jesus spoke these words, recorded in Matthew 25:40, He was describing those who would populate the kingdom of God....Mary Ashley exhibited for us what our Lord was teaching. That her actions were forever directed toward 'one of the least of these.' And those actions were not from a motive that was ulterior, sordid, or filled with duplicity. I prayed that God would grant me such a quality of spirit."

Jim's beautiful tribute to my sister speaks of a servant heart. That was Mary Ashley. A servant—a woman who gave herself away to everyone she met.

The least of these....I thought about all the people whose lives she had touched. The garbage collector who heard Mary Ashley's enthusiastic appreciation when she stopped her car and got out to thank him for keeping the streets of Charleston clean. The lunchroom worker who complimented my sister on the dress she was wearing, then received that same dress as a gift after Mary Ashley hurried home to change. The kitchen staff at the country club, who left their posts when they heard Mary Ashley was there to tell her how much they loved her—one last time. When we minister to the least of these, we minister to the Lord.

This is the goal mature women are striving to attain. Finally to reach the heights—of servanthood. It's what Jesus taught us most eloquently through His life and sacrificial death. That "The Best" we are seeking comes when we lay down all that we have and are on this earth.

There were so many others my sister blessed during her short time on this earth. Not just the down-and-outers, but the up-and-outers. Like the young lawyer who had disgraced his name, left his wife and child, and been spurned by many in town, only to run into Mary Ashley on his first day of practice. "I was a cad," he confessed to me, weeping near the open casket of my sister as we received condolence calls. "I was wild and young and irresponsible. My ex-wife was one of your sister's best friends, so Mary Ashley had no reason to forgive me...." By now he was sobbing openly. "But you know what she said that day? It changed my whole life. She said, 'Welcome home,' and gave me a big hug."

When you reach the gates of heaven, our Lord Jesus will be there to welcome you Home. He will not receive you on the basis of your bank book or the physical beauty you have been able to maintain. Not the number of friends in your social circle or your charitable works and kind deeds. Not on how many degrees you have earned or how many houses you have decorated or what earthly empire you have built. He will look in the Lamb's Book of Life, and finding your name written in His own blood will say, *"Forgiven. 'Well done, good and faithful servant....Enter into the joy of your lord'"* (Matthew 25:21 NKJV).

Just think of stepping on shore and finding it heaven!

Of touching a hand and finding it God's!

Of breathing new air and finding it celestial!

Of waking up in glory and finding it home!

Words © by L. E. Singer and Don Wyrtzen. Music © by Don Wyrtzen.

Other Books by
Ann Platz

❧

The Pleasure of Your Company

Experts on hospitality Ann Platz and Susan Wales introduce easy and enjoyable ways to pamper guests and develop a unique personal signature for every social situation. Delicious menus and recipes are provided for effortless entertaining. Elegant artwork draped in soft colors plays centerpiece to ideas for setting tables and moods that are appropriate to each occasion, and suggestions for adding pizazz to your presentation.

Social Graces

This fun and fabulous course in old-fashioned manners reclaims genuine hospitality for today's busy lives. Against a backdrop of luxurious paintings, find etiquette gems as you learn to put people at ease with graceful manners, cultivate the art of conversation, influence others with good cheer, and create a personal, heartfelt style.

The Blessing

Gracious Father,

I pray that each person who reads this book will come into the full knowledge of Your unlimited love, Your vast compassion, and Your comforting truths.

Please give each one of these precious new friends enthusiasm for their homes, creativity for their lives, and the ability to see You in others as they grow and mature in You.

Quicken them, Lord, to know Your will. Make us all good listeners, as well as gracious speakers.

We pray for quiet moments of reflection and respite from life's busy pace. Guide our restless thoughts and give us courage to overcome. Fill us with Your Spirit. Thank You for new beginnings and for Your healing love.

As these women of wisdom receive wholeness, lead them out into the world to be instruments of truth and beauty, that their lives may reflect Your glory. And in due time, take them Home—to Your House.

In Jesus' name, Amen.

Notes

1. B. J. Hoff, *Faces in the Crowd* (Anderson, IN: Warner Press, 1993)

2. B. J. Hoff, *Thorns and Thrones*, (Anderson, IN: Warner Press, 1991)

About the Author

Warm, hospitable, and gracious, Ann Platz epitomizes the qualities that people most admire about the South. Raised with a deep appreciation for the art of beautiful living, she grew up in an ancestral plantation home in Orangeburg, South Carolina. Ann moved to Atlanta, Georgia, in the mid-70s, where she resides with her husband, John. She is the mother of two daughters, Courtney Cloer Norton and Margo Fitzgerald Cloer. Together, she and John have six grandchildren.

Ann has been well known in the South as an interior designer for over twenty-five years and is a popular and delightful lecturer. Speaking on topics from love and marriage to design and etiquette, Ann warms the heart with her effortless southern elegance and storytelling wit.

She is the author of six other books, including *Social Graces* and *The Pleasure of Your Company,* with Harvest House Publishers. Her design credentials include a governor's mansion, country clubs, historic houses, as well as two Southern Living Idea Houses. She and John are members of Mount Paran Church of God. They are active in the Christian community of Greater Atlanta.

Dear Friends,

Please write to me and let me know how this book has impacted your life. I want to encourage you to allow God's transforming grace to work for you. I would love to hear from you. Also, I am available to speak to church and other groups.

Blessings,
Ann

Ann Platz
1266 West Paces Ferry Road
#521
Atlanta, Georgia 30327-2306
(Fax) 404-237-3810
(E-Mail) annplatz@flash.net